Treasures of the
Fitzwilliam Museum

Treasures of the Fitzwilliam Museum

An illustrated souvenir
of the collections

Sponsored by Barclays Bank

P̶P The Pevensey Press
Published for
Fitzwilliam Museum Enterprises Ltd
Cambridge England

Front cover: The Fitzwilliam Museum's grandiloquent portico on Trumpington Street prefaces the original building, designed by George Basevi (1794–1845) and begun in 1836. The University selected his plans from thirty-six competing schemes, both classical and gothic.

Back cover: The Museum's sombrely magnificent entrance hall. The original design was modified by C.R.Cockerell, who supervised construction after Basevi was killed in a fall from scaffolding inside Ely Cathedral. The decoration was completed by E.M.Barry (1870–5). Masterpieces of late 18th- and early 19th-century sculpture are displayed here; the focus of the stair-well is the original, untinted *Venus Verticordia* by John Gibson (1790–1866).

Frontispiece: Joseph Wright of Derby (1734–97): *The Hon. Richard Fitzwilliam, later 7th Viscount Fitzwilliam of Merrion, Founder of the Fitzwilliam Museum,* oil on canvas, 74.3×62.2cm. Richard Fitzwilliam (1745–1816) was admitted to Trinity Hall, Cambridge, in 1761. This portrait was painted in 1764 for Samuel Hallifax, fellow and tutor of Trinity Hall and private tutor to Fitzwilliam (who stood godfather to his son). Fitzwilliam is shown wearing the gown of an undergraduate fellow-commoner, of the kind worn by noblemen on special occasions. He succeeded his father as 7th Viscount in 1776 and inherited the family seat at Mount Merrion, near Dublin. He lived principally in England, at Fitzwilliam House in Richmond, Surrey. He died unmarried, leaving his library and collections of paintings and prints to the University of Cambridge, together with £100,000 to build a museum to house them (opened 1848). His land and titles went to his two brothers successively; both died childless, and in 1833 the family and titles became extinct.

Published by The Pevensey Press
6 De Freville Avenue, Cambridge CB4 1HR, UK
for Fitzwilliam Museum Enterprises Ltd

Photographs by Andrew Morris and James Butler (Fitzwilliam Museum Photographic Department), except 15, 22, 37, 40, 98 and 99 (Department of Coins and Medals), and front cover, by Ernest Frankl (Pevensey Press).

Introduction by Michael Hall (Pevensey Press); captions compiled by Michael Hall in association with the Keepers: J.G.Pollard (Coins and Medals); R.V.Nicholls (Antiquities); R.A.Crighton (Applied Arts); P.Woudhuysen (Manuscripts and Printed Books); E.C.Chamberlain (Prints); D.E.Scrase (Paintings and Drawings); and Assistant Keepers: T.R.Volk (Coins and Medals); Miss J.Bourriau (Antiquities); Miss J.E.Poole (Applied Arts).

The publishers gratefully acknowledge the generous assistance of Professor Michael Jaffé, Director, and of the Museum staff named above, in the preparation of this book. Responsibility for any errors remains with the publishers.

Edited by Ruth Smith
Designed by Tim McPhee in association with The Pevensey Press
Design and production in association with Book Production Consultants, Cambridge
© The Fitzwilliam Museum, © The Pevensey Press

First published 1982   Reprinted 1986

ISBN 0 907115 13 6 hard covers
ISBN 0 907115 14 4 paperback

Typesetting in Baskerville by Westholme Graphics Ltd
Printed in Hong Kong

Dimensions of objects illustrated
Dimensions are given in the order: height, width, depth; coins and medals are reproduced to actual size. Abbreviations: H height W width L length D diameter.

Foreword

Thanks to its Founder, a rich amateur of European music and painting and prints, and to a succession of benefactors offering by gift or bequest a vast range of distinguished and desirable things, the Fitzwilliam is indeed a treasure house. For many hundreds of thousands of visitors it is also the finest small museum in Western Europe. The Friends of the Fitzwilliam support acquisitions by entrusting the sum of their subscriptions to the Director of the day. The Syndicate, which watches over all the affairs of the Museum on behalf of the University, has the income from various trust funds at its disposal for purchases, strengthened by a modest allocation of funds, determined annually, from the University Chest. The funds available for well-judged purchases can be matched, up to certain limits, by grants from the Fund for the Regions, administered by the Victoria and Albert Museum, also supplemented on occasion by the National Art-Collections Fund, by the Pilgrim Trust and by other generous bodies. Yet the shortage of current funds under the Museum's control, not least for publication of these great and growing collections, remains acute.

It is particularly welcome that substantial support is now forthcoming from the University's bankers, Barclays Bank, to assist the publication of a selection of the Museum's treasures in a form and at a price which can reach a wide public. *The Fitzwilliam Museum: An Illustrated Survey*, a lavish production published by the Trianon Press in 1958 with funds provided by the late Guy Knowles, has long been out of print. *Treasures of the Fitzwilliam Museum* is not written by the Director as the earlier volume quite distinctively was. Nevertheless, the publishers, in choosing what to reproduce and in writing the accompanying captions, have consulted members of the Museum's curatorial staff and myself. In putting this book together outside the Museum, but with inside access – notably to the Museum's highly skilled photographic services – the Pevensey Press has worked in an eminently worthwhile cause, that of bringing the Fitzwilliam closer to a yet more extensive public.

Michael Jaffé
Director

Introduction

The Fitzwilliam, which houses the University of Cambridge collections of art and antiquities, is one of the oldest public museums in the country. It was founded in 1816 by Richard, 7th Viscount Fitzwilliam of Merrion (see frontispiece), who bequeathed pictures, books, manuscripts and prints to the University 'for the purpose of promoting the increase of learning and the other great objects of that noble Foundation', together with money to build a museum to house them. The Founder's collections reflect the tastes of English connoisseurs of his time: he liked Venetian paintings (**44–6**, **77**), Dutch paintings, prints (his collection of Rembrandt etchings was the finest in England), medieval illuminated manuscripts and, especially, music (**50**).

A competition for a design for the building was won by George Basevi in 1834; the foundation stone was laid in 1837, and the Museum opened in 1848. For most of the 19th century it remained a backwater of Cambridge academic life. Members of the public, if 'respectably dressed', were admitted on three days of the week; on other days the Museum was open to University members 'in Academical Habit' alone. Victorian guidebooks suggest a disordered collection in which masterpieces were hung next to curiosities such as models of the Taj Mahal and boxes of Indian crabs. Excitement was caused by the Vice Chancellor's rehanging of the pictures to make the Palma Vecchio and Titian's *Venus* (**45**, **46**) less obvious ('the exhibition of nude figures in a public gallery is always a matter of some embarrassment') and, in June 1864, by a ball in the Museum to entertain the Prince and Princess of Wales. However, important gifts and bequests were received: for example, in 1861 Ruskin presented 25 Turner watercolours (including **90**) – 'more fashionable as a unique style of Art than pleasing to many of our visitors', commented a guidebook of 1868; in 1873 the Rev. R. E. Kerrich gave several pictures including the Joos van Cleve (**41**); and in 1879 Joseph Prior gave the Frans Hals (**62**). The few important purchases, from severely limited University funds, included Colonel Leake's classical antiquities in 1864 (**12**, **13**) and Charles Butler's early Italian paintings (including the Simone Martini, **31**).

The first director, Sidney Colvin, was appointed in 1876 and systematic development of the collections began, tentatively at first. The directorship of M. R. James (1893–1908) was notable for his catalogue of the Museum's medieval manuscripts, in which he also appealed for gifts and bequests. He was answered by the magnificent bequest in 1904 of Frank McClean's collection of manuscripts, books, enamels and ivories (e.g. **28**). This was closely followed by a series of gifts of ancient coins, including 10,000 Greek, from McClean's brother, John (e.g. **15c**).

No director has had a greater influence on the history of the Museum than S. C. Cockerell, who between 1908 and 1937 transformed the Museum and its collections; he commented, 'I found it a pig stye, I turned it into a palace.' In 1909 he founded the Friends of the Fitzwilliam, the first organisation of its kind in the country, to raise money for purchases (amongst many others, **9**, **10**, **14**, **35**, **73**, **98**, **100**, **115**). In 1912 C. B. Marlay bequeathed a large and miscellaneous collection (including **39** and **63**) and money to house it, which allowed Cockerell to build the first extension (opened 1924) and rearrange the Museum in a fashion taken for granted today, but then revolutionary. The pictures were rehung in a single or double line; the antiquities were ordered in a logical fashion; and the upper galleries were transformed by the addition of oriental carpets, English and other antique furniture, wallcases of ceramics, and flowers. As many visitors have found, the resulting impression is of the public apartments of a stately home.

Cockerell assiduously pursued potential benefactors (it was said that his appearance at the sickbed of the rich was a sure sign of an imminent death), enabling the Courtauld Galleries to be built in 1931 and the Henderson Galleries and Charrington Print Room in 1936. He also attracted purchasing funds to a Museum which had received no money bequests since the Founder's. In addition he and his successors have been aided by outside bodies. Apart from occasional spectacular purchases such as Van Dyck's *Virgin and Child* (**58**, acquired after a public appeal in 1976), and Stubbs' *Gimcrack with John Pratt up, on Newmarket Heath* (acquired after a public appeal in 1982), the Fitzwilliam's resources

The Museum in 1887: a photograph taken in Gallery III (now devoted chiefly to a conspectus of British art from the 16th to the early 19th century) to commemorate the fiftieth anniversary of the laying of the foundation stone. The two gowned figures are (centre) Charles Waldstein, Director 1883–9, and (right) M.R. James, Director 1893–1908; they are surrounded by the Museum's staff. The portrait is of the Founder, copied after Henry Howard. The photograph shows how differently the picture galleries were arranged in the 19th century, with crowded walls and empty floors. The pictures visible here include Paolo Veronese's 'Hermes, Herse and Aglauros' and Titian's 'Venus and Cupid with a Luteplayer', nos. 44 and 46 in this book.

never allow it the ambitious purchasing policy of a national collection. It has been shaped – and this is a large part of its charm – by gifts, so that its collections display the changing tastes of English connoisseurs since the 18th century. In this century Charles Fairfax Murray (*d*1919) gave paintings by Titian (**47**), Gainsborough (**80**) and Hogarth (**84**); James Glaisher, a fellow of Trinity, bequeathed a large collection of ceramics in 1928 (e.g. **67**); the artist Charles Shannon bequeathed in 1937 the distinguished collection of art and antiquities he had formed with his friend Charles Ricketts (e.g. **2**, **75**, and see **112**); Oscar Raphael bequeathed Near Eastern and oriental antiquities and works of art in 1941 (e.g. **4**, **24–6**); Major R. G. and Colonel T. G. Gayer-Anderson gave a large collection of Egyptian antiquities in 1942–9 (e.g. **6**); the bequest of Louis Clarke, director of the Museum 1937–46, was particularly rich in drawings (**33**, **59**, **60**); and in 1967 Henry Broughton, 2nd Lord Fairhaven, gave an extensive collection of flower paintings and drawings (e.g. **72**, **87**). Such examples of rich benefactions represent only part of the expansion of the collections, which has necessitated the building of two further extensions (1966 and 1975). These include a gallery for contemporary art and the Adeane Gallery for temporary exhibitions, both indications of the vitality of a modern museum devoted – as its Founder desired – to 'the increase of learning', and bringing pleasure to all who live in or visit Cambridge.

▲ **1** *Reindeer*, incised on limestone, L 70mm, and *Burin*, flint, L 57mm, both Paleolithic, *c*12000 BC, from Laugerie Basse. The earliest drawings in the Fitzwilliam are a small number of incised sketches dating from the Magdalenian V–VI Periods, found in the Dordogne; they came to the Museum from the collection of the noted Cambridge prehistorian Miles Burkitt. This small masterpiece showing a trotting reindeer looking over its shoulder demonstrates the skill of the artist in capturing animal forms and movement. (Reindeer inhabited France during the Paleolithic period.) The contemporary burin from the same region is the sort of tool that was used to incise this drawing.

► **2** *An Official*, plastered and painted wood, H 550mm, Egyptian, Dynasty VI (*c*23rd century BC). The staff in his hand is restored; probably there was originally a sceptre of office in his other hand. Though he is an adult, there is an attachment on the right of his head for the side-lock of a child, which would have been worn either as a mark of filiation (if the statue was placed in his father's tomb), or to denote membership of a special priesthood. The layer of gesso (fine plaster) was applied to cover the grain and other faults in the wood and provide an even ground for painting. This splendid tomb figure of the late Old Kingdom was bequeathed by the artists C.S.Ricketts and C.H.Shannon.

◄ **3** *Cartonnage of Nekhtefmut*, linen pulp, plastered and painted, with wooden strengthening at beard and feet and inlaid glass eyes and beard, H 1783mm, Egyptian, *c*891 BC. The tomb of Nekhtefmut and his wife, found within the precincts of the mortuary temple of Ramesses II at Thebes, was excavated by Sir W.M.Flinders Petrie and J.E.Quibell in 1896. The cartonnage, which closely follows the form of the wrapped mummified body that it covered, was found inside Nekhtefmut's innermost wooden coffin. Leather trappings on the mummy carried the names and title of King Osorkon I (*c*924–889 BC) and the mummy's wrappings carry the dates 'Year 33' (presumably of Osorkon I) and 'Year 3' (presumably of Senoschis II, Osorkon's co-regent in his last years and his prospective successor, though in the event he died first). The main inscription on the front of the cartonnage gives Nekhtefmut's titles as 'beloved divine father, opener of the two doors of heaven [i.e. the inner shrine] of the Temple of Amūn at Karnak' and adds the names of his ancestors to four generations. It is inscribed on the back with texts from the *Book of the Dead* (the Egyptian collection of spells and prayers for the afterlife). The back of the cartonnage was split open by the excavators and the mummy was removed and unwrapped. A posy, scarabs and amulets placed on the body are on display in the Museum.

➤**4** *Ammenemes III*, shelly limestone, H 120mm, Egyptian, Dynasty XII. Ammenemes III was Pharaoh between 1842 and 1797 BC and is chiefly remembered for completing the draining of the Faiyûm – converting it into the richest farmland in Egypt – and for his vast funerary temple complex, the 'Labyrinth' near Crocodilopolis described by Herodotus (II,148). This portrait of the young ruler is known as the Oscar Raphael head after its former owner, who bequeathed it to the Museum. It shows how Egyptian sculptors of the late Middle Kingdom achieved a ruthless, almost brutal realism in rendering the human likeness.

▲ **5** *Scene from the Inner Coffin of Espawershefi*, wood, plastered and painted, coffin 1900×600×490mm. Espawershefi was head of the scribes of the great temple of Amūn at Karnak, Thebes, during the later part of Dynasty XXI (i.e. *c*980–940 BC). He was thus an important and wealthy official, able to command the finest craftsmen of his time, as the quality of his set of coffins confirms. His mummy was laid under a wooden anthropoid cover and encased in two coffins. The inner coffin has been cleaned and its flaking paint replaced in position; the paint and the varnish are entirely original. The scene, like most of those on Espawershefi's coffins, is concerned with his journey through the Netherworld. On either side the deceased, dressed in his finest white linen, is shown kneeling, his arms raised in adoration below the image of his personal god, Amūn-Re, chief deity of Thebes – here shown in the guise of a ram. In the centre are the gods of earth, sky and air. The sky goddess Nut frames the scene, making an arc of her body; she is supported by Shu, god of the air. Reclining below them, coloured green for fertility, is Geb, god of the earth. The hieroglyphic texts identify the gods and call on them to ensure the rebirth of Espawershefi in the next world. The coffins were given to the University in 1822 by two intrepid clergymen, George Waddington and Barnard Hanbury, fellows of Trinity College, who visited Egypt and the Sudan in 1821 shortly after Napoleon's expedition, when Egypt was at last opening to a fascinated Europe.

▼ **6** (left) *Owl*, limestone flake, 145×95mm, and (right) *Unshaven stonemason*, limestone flake, 150×135mm, both Egyptian, *c*13th–12th centuries BC. In ancient Egypt papyrus was too expensive a material to be used for everyday jottings; for these or for preliminary designs or for simple doodling people used pottery sherds or flattish limestone flakes. A large number of such ephemeral documents has survived at Deir el-Medîna, the workmen's village near Thebes, where the stonemasons, painters and sculptors who decorated the royal tombs lived. Many of these fragments are painters' sketches or sculptors' trial pieces. The collection of them in the Fitzwilliam is perhaps the most important in any British museum, and it allows us to glimpse behind the formal art of Egypt the everyday lives of the men who created it. The burly, bald-headed stonemason has been rapidly sketched, ear-ringed and stubble-chinned, as he toils with his round-headed mallet and chisel. The owl is a painter's study for the hieroglyphic sign 'm'; although the form was conventional, the artist has taken some trouble to reproduce the pattern of the feathers of (probably) a barn owl.

▲ **7** *Bull*, ivory, 56×72mm, Phoenician, 8th century BC. This finely carved little panel formed part of a frieze showing cattle filing past. Its well-finished back suggests that it formed part of the side of a small cylindrical pyxis or casket, although similar friezes are also attested on massive furniture legs. It was excavated in Fort Shalmaneser at Nimrud (Calah) near the River Tigris by Professor Sir Max Mallowan working on behalf of the British School of Archaeology in Iraq. Nimrud became an Assyrian royal capital in 879 BC with the completion of the palace of King Ashurnaṣirpal II (the source of the splendid gypsum reliefs in the Fitzwilliam). Fort Shalmaneser was erected as a royal residence *c*846 BC by Ashurnaṣirpal's successor, Shalmaneser III, but was later converted to a fortress and arsenal. In the 8th century BC an abundance of richly carved ivory furniture and other items reached Nimrud from Syria and Phoenicia as booty and tribute; in 614 BC, when Nimrud itself was destroyed, much of it was being stored in Fort Shalmaneser.

► **8** *Roaring Lion*, bronze, H 560mm, S Arabian, *c*700 BC. This ferocious sculpture is the fore-part of a statue fitted around a massive door-jamb, and was almost certainly one of a pair flanking a major gateway. It was found in the Wadi al-Quatr and brought to Shibam in the Hadramaut (now in the Democratic Republic of the Yemen). It is one of the earliest surviving hollow cast bronze statues and was fashioned by the lost-wax process, the front and side of the sculpture being made separately and the side being cast on to the front. Part of the casting core still survives inside. The bronze is remarkable for its high lead content, added deliberately to facilitate the flow of the molten metal. The present left ear is an ancient replacement, its predecessor having presumably been knocked off by a vehicle passing through the gateway. This statue is the earliest known work of a native school of bronze sculpture in S Arabia. The idea of gate-lions seems to be derived from N Syria, and the style of the bronze lion itself is closely modelled on that of N Syrian stone sculptures of the later 8th century BC. It was presented by an Arab chief to Lt Col. the Hon. M.T.Boscawen, in whose memory it was given to the Museum.

9 *Cluster Vase*, pottery, H 289mm, Early Cycladic III, *c*2000 BC. This simply painted multiple vase dates from near the end of the Early Cycladic civilisation, which appears to have exercised maritime control over the Aegean for over 1000 years, and whose craftsmen were exceptionally skilled in pottery, simple metallurgy and carving vases and figures of marble. Its shape is known by the later Greek name of *kernos* which, strictly speaking, refers to much later vessels of similar form connected in classical times with the cult of Demeter and similar deities. The function of the extremely rare Cycladic examples is unknown, but since they appear to be from tombs, it is presumed to be connected with funerary ritual.

10 *Girl*, terracotta, H 237mm, Attic, Round Group, *c*500–490 BC. When the Persian armies sacked Athens in 480 BC and destroyed the temples on the Acropolis they inadvertently preserved, broken and buried, the beautiful marble statues dedicated to Athena and known as *korai* (girls). On the Acropolis and at the other sanctuaries of Attica they also smashed a larger number of much smaller *korai* of terracotta, which now mostly survive only in fragments. This smiling girl is one of the few intact examples, being possibly from a grave rather than a sanctuary. As usual in Athens at this date, she was fashioned almost solid in a simple one-piece clay mould.

▲ **11** *Bell-krater*, pottery, with red-figure decoration, H 150mm, Boeotian, *c*420 BC. Red-figure wares have the background painted black and the figures reserved, leaving the red clay exposed. This very fine example is an exceptionally small mixing-bowl for wine. It shows the sea-nymph Thetis on a hippocamp (a sea-monster with the fore-parts of a horse), bringing the shield made by Hephaestus for her son, Achilles, to replace the armour lent to Patroclus and seized by Hector. (See the elaborate account of the forging of the shield in *Iliad* XVIII, which inspired the English neoclassic artist John Flaxman (1775–1826) to make a shield after Homer's description; one of the three examples he cast is in the Fitzwilliam.) This vase is one of the most outstanding achievements of the Boeotian red-figure potters, who naturally drew much of their inspiration from the far more prolific potters of neighbouring Attica.

◄13 *Engraved Gem*, sapphirine chalcedony scaraboid, 22×17×8mm, E Greek, c450–440 BC (enlarged × 3). Dexamenos of Chios is regarded as the greatest classical Greek seal engraver. One of four surviving signed gems from his hand, this seal is exceptionally innovative and experimental, e.g. in its attempt at base-line perspective in rendering the backless chair in which the principal figure sits – not wholly successful to our eyes but daring and new when the stone was cut. It was carved for a woman, and is inscribed 'belonging to Mikē'. A lady is shown attended by a servant girl carrying a mirror and a garland.

▼14 *Youths with Hoops*, Pentelic marble, W 483mm, Attic, c330 BC. This charming grave relief represents the neck and handles of a tall *loutrophoros*, an elongated pottery or metal vessel for bringing water to the bridal bath. In 4th-century-BC Athens the custom arose of erecting marble *loutrophoroi* over the graves of those who died unmarried. This is the best example known of the very rare ones with relief figures at the handles, presumably inspired by actual statuettes on the lost metal vessels in this form. The inverted scale pattern of the neck, banded with bead-and-reel ornament, suggests the trunk of a stylised palm tree, its fronds spreading out to support a broad mouth.

◄12 *Neck-amphora*, pottery with black-figure decoration in the manner of the Lysippides Painter, H 305mm, Attic, c530–520 BC. Black-figure pottery is decorated with figures painted in silhouette on the red pottery ground, details being added by incision. This delicately painted vase, found at Vulci in Italy, is from the collection of the great Greek topographer Lt Col. W.M.Leake. It shows five satyrs dancing energetically: one provides the music on his double flute, another carries a heavy skin of wine, a third bears the krater for mixing it with water and the pitcher for dispensing it, and the leader seems to be holding the *phiale* (shallow dish) for pouring a libation before feasting begins. Satyrs, with their horses' tails and ears and their irrepressible animality, appear suddenly in Greek art in the 6th century BC in connection with the orgiastic worship of the god Dionysos.

a b

c d e

f g h

▲ 15 *Ancient Coins.* By tradition the Lydians of Asia Minor were the first people to strike gold and silver coins, in the 6th century BC. Examples in both metals [*a*, silver] closely resemble certain of the earliest Greek coins struck in electrum, a natural alloy of gold and silver. The use of coin was quickly established throughout the Greek world. Even in small communities the quality of the engraving could be very high, as in the case of the elegant coinage struck at Sicilian Naxos in the 5th century BC [*c*]. In the 4th century Alexander the Great carried Greek coinage to the East. From the independent Hellenistic kingdom in Afghanistan and the Punjab came a remarkable series portraying earlier Greek rulers of Bactria and India [*d*]. More remotely derived from Greek prototypes, above all from the coins of Alexander's father, Philip II, are the Iron Age coinages of Central Europe, including those of pre-conquest Britain, e.g. the gold *stater* of Antedios from the Lakenheath hoard [*b*].

The coinage of Rome long abjured the life portraiture characteristic of contemporary

Hellenistic issues, with its regal or tyrannical overtones. The first living Roman to be portrayed on the Republic's coins was Julius Caesar, who set a pattern for the coming Empire. On perhaps the most celebrated Roman coin, even Caesar's assassin Brutus combined the symbols of liberation from tyranny with his own portrait [*f*]. During the first three centuries of the Empire coins were struck at Rome, but also at small local mints with local types. The best surviving representation of the celebrated cult statue of Zeus at Olympia by the classical sculptor Pheidias occurs on an issue of the Greek city of Elis [*e*]. By contrast, the later Roman coinage, struck at mints throughout the Empire, is uniform and highly stylised. Thus the coinage of the usurper Maximus, probably the last issue of Roman Britain, preserves the standard reverse type of the contemporary western mints with an imperial bust that lacks true individuality [*g*]. The gold coinage of the Empire's powerful eastern neighbour, the Sassanian monarchy of Iran, appears to have been largely ceremonial. The spectacular 'solidus' of

Khusru II exhibits on the reverse a female bust within a nimbus of flames, presumably a representation of the goddess Anahita [h].

◄ [a] Lydia, Croesus (560–45 BC) (?), Sardis, silver *stater*: foreparts of lion and bull/two incuse squares; [b] Britain, Iceni, Antedios (cAD 35–45), uncertain East Anglian mint, red gold *stater*: three crescents/horse; [c] Sicily, Naxos, c430 BC, silver *tetradrachm*: head of Dionysus/squatting Silenus; [d] India, Agathocles (c171–60 BC), Pushkalavati, silver *tetradrachm*: head of Antiochus I/Zeus; [e] Peloponnese, Elis, Olympia, AD 134/5, bronze issue: bust of Hadrian/head of Zeus after statue by Pheidias; [f] Roman Republic, Brutus (with L. Plaetorius Cestianus), uncertain eastern mint, c42 BC, silver *denarius*: head of Brutus/*pileus* ('Liberty cap') between two daggers, EID.MAR ('Ides of March'); [g] Roman Empire, Magnus Maximus (AD 383–8), London, gold *solidus*: bust of Maximus/Victory above two emperors; [h] Sassanian Empire, Khusru II (AD 591–628), Ctesiphon, year 21, gold 'solidus': bust of Khusru/ bust of Anahita.

▼ **16** *The Pashley Sarcophagus* (detail), Luna marble, H of main frieze 491mm, cAD 130–50. This is a detail from what is perhaps the finest Roman sarcophagus in the country and one remarkable also as an Italian work found in Greece. It was made in Rome itself and used for a burial at Arvi, on the S coast of Crete. It depicts the triumphal return from India of Bacchus (Dionysos), god of wine, with his retinue of satyrs and maenads. This detail, from near the head of the procession, shows an elephant (the artist inappropriately chose an African species) guided by a young satyr who sits on its back and uses his throwing-stick as a goad. He is conversing with a maenad who reclines on the elephant's shoulder and holds a *thyrsos* and a *kantharos* (the staff and drinking-vessel of the followers of Bacchus); she rests her *kantharos* on a *cista*, the kind of lidded basket sacred to the Bacchic rites. A young satyr, also with a *kantharos*, sits beside her, and on the haunches of the elephant is another maenad, blowing a double pipe. Behind the elephant is a superbly carved fragmentary satyr holding a *thyrsos* and panther skin and carrying a satyr child. The sarcophagus, given to the Museum by Admiral Sir Pulteney Malcolm in 1835, derives its name from its first publication in Robert Pashley's *Travels in Crete* (1837).

◄ **17** *Fountain Niche*, coloured glass tesserae, shells, marble inlays, 1121×794mm, Roman, *c* mid 1st century AD. Apsidal niches were associated with fountains in the small peristyle gardens of Roman town houses and seem to have originated as shell grottoes, of which the shells edging the mosaic here are a vestige. This niche is from Baiae, near Naples; others are known from Rome, Pompeii and Herculaneum. Its garden theme may be derived from the wall-paintings of the underground Garden Room of the Villa of Livia at Primaporta, Rome (now in the Museo Nazionale Romano). Niches such as this mark the beginnings of wall (as opposed to floor) mosaics, which later became a major Byzantine art form.

►**18** *Part of a Couch*, carved bone (over restored wood with iron fittings), H 840mm, Roman, *c*30–20 BC. This entered the Fitzwilliam as hundreds of pieces of richly carved bone. Its foot end has been restored and painstakingly reconstructed by the Museum's staff, revealing it as a piece of ancient furniture of unprecedented elaboration and quality. It belongs to a small group of couches covered with carved bone, made in the northern part of central Italy between the 1st century BC and the 1st century AD. The winged female who forms part of the legs represents Turan, the Etruscan equivalent of Venus; at her shoulder is Cupid and at her feet a goose. Reliefs on the frame show Apollo playing his lyre; above are medallions with profile reliefs of Cupid. In all the documented finds such couches

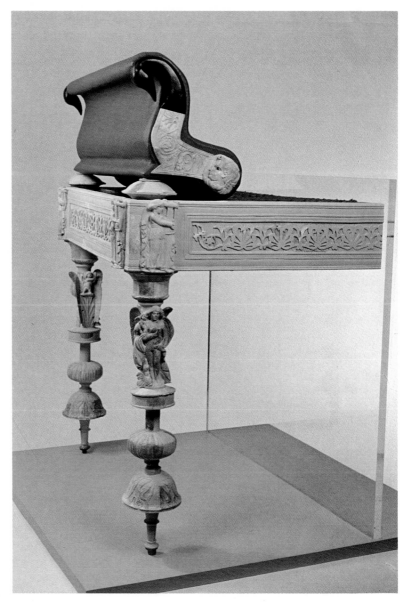

served as biers in tombs or are associated with cremation burials. But they bear no funerary imagery, so in the lifetime of their owners they may have filled a quite different role, possibly as the Roman *lectus genialis*, the bed associated with marriage and domestic religious rites.

◄ 19 *Flask with 'Snake-Thread' Decoration*, blown glass with applied coiled base ring, H 242mm, Syrian, *c* end of 2nd century AD. This splendid flask was found in a tomb at Marion (now Polis tis Khrysokhou) in Cyprus. Its decoration was achieved by trailing molten glass over the blown body of the vessel and tooling and shaping it while still soft. After the invention of glass-blowing in the 1st century BC, glass-working centres flourished in various parts of the Roman world. In the east some of the best were along the Syro-Phoenician coast, where mould-blown glass was developed; in the west the greatest were in the Rhine valley, notably at Cologne. This is part of the small amount of 'snake-thread' glass known to be Syrian. The technique soon ended in the east, apparently because the craftsmen emigrated to the Rhineland, where 'snake-thread' suddenly appeared and flourished for a long period.

◄ 20 *Jupiter*, terracotta, H 157mm, Roman, 1st–2nd century AD. This head beautifully conveys the brooding dignity of a great god of classical antiquity. Its identification rests partly on iconographic links with other works and partly on the testimony of its excavators who, having apparently found elements of the body as well as the head, unhesitatingly named the figure as Zeus, or Jupiter. It was discovered in 1884 at the ancient Lanuvium (now Lanuvio or Città Lavinia), in what was mistakenly known as the 'Villa of Caligula', a massive complex apparently associated with marble sculptures of the mid and late 2nd century AD. Roman terracotta sculpture for the adornment of buildings seems to have achieved its finest expression at the beginning of the Imperial period when an older, largely Etruscan tradition fused with powerful new influences from Greece. This Jupiter may be an earlier work dating from this period and re-installed at the villa or a remarkably fresh, early-looking 2nd-century creation specially commissioned for decoration of one of the villa buildings.

▼ **22** *Mogul Coin*, Akbar (1556–1605), Agra Town, 981AH (AD1573/4), gold *muhar*: Profession of Faith and names of the four orthodox caliphs/name and titles of Akbar. With rare exceptions Mogul coins, like other Mohammedan issues, are non-pictorial; instead of types they carry the Profession of Faith (*Kalima*), the name and the conventional, often elaborate, titles of the ruler, and the date and place of striking. The decorative possibilities of the Persian script are, however, exploited to achieve designs of great harmony and beauty. For certain extremely rare issues of the Emperor Akbar, of which this is one, the effect is enhanced by fashioning the ends of the coin to resemble the arch of a prayer-niche or *mihrab*.

▲ **21** *Turkey*, body colour with gold, 208×137mm, Mogul, period of Jahangir (1605–27). During Jahangir's reign it became common to paint actual portraits of animals and birds – a vogue which paralleled increasing interest in human portraiture. This turkey is probably the same as the one in the Victoria and Albert Museum, painted by Ustad Mansur.

▶23 *Vishnu*, bronze with incised decoration, gilt and set with gemstones, H 400mm, Nepalese, *c*1200–1400 or earlier. In Hindu mythology Vishnu is, with Brahma and Siva, one of the supreme trinity of the gods. He is a gigantic youth who crosses the heavens in three strides, symbolising the course of the sun. He is usually depicted, as in this splendid sculpture, with four arms holding the lotus seed of creation, the wheel of life and death, the mace that destroys illusion and the conch shell on which the primordial noise is sounded. The statue may originally have been part of a group with Vishnu's consort, Sri Lakshmi, and Garuda, his bird-man steed; it had a base and an aureole which were cast separately and are now lost. The bronze is heavily patinated, which suggests that it was buried at some time. The mace has been bent to the left, perhaps in the course of the probably accidental excavation.

◄ **25** *Box*, celadon glazed stoneware, H 80mm, Chinese, Yüeh ware, T'ang dynasty (AD 618–906), 9th–10th century. This was probably made in the Shang-lin-hu region, one of the most celebrated centres of the stoneware named after the Chekiang kingdom of Yüeh (SE China), where it was first produced. The finest 10th-century examples are said to have been made exclusively for the Yüeh princes and were called *pi-sê yao*, 'reserved colour ware' (i.e. reserved for the court). The subtle green is produced by minute amounts of iron in the glaze and by firing in an oxygen-starved atmosphere. The double lotus shape of this box probably derives from a gold or silver example; the lotus suggests a Buddhist use, perhaps as an incense container.

◄ **24** *Buffalo*, green jade (nephrite), L 432mm, Chinese, Ming dynasty (1368–1644). Jade, principally nephrite and jadeite, is a hard, tough and fibrous stone, laborious to work, ranging in colour from milky white through yellow and green to black. In China it has been revered from the Stone Age to the present day. Amuletic powers and the capacity to prevent corruption are attributed to it, hence its occurrence in grave furniture, e.g. funerary suits. It was particularly associated with the imperial family. Until 1900 this buffalo was part of the furnishings of the Winter Palace in Peking, together with a black jade horse and a white 'dragon-horse' (both also in the Fitzwilliam). All three were removed during the aftermath of the Boxer Rising and auctioned at the British Legation. Palace tradition attributed the buffalo and the black horse to the Han dynasty (206 BC – AD 220), and held that the Yung-lo emperor (1403–24) brought them to Peking *c*1420. The 'dragon-horse' was reputedly commissioned by the K'ang-hsi emperor (1662–1722) to complement the other two. Scholars now believe that the buffalo is of Ming date and probably postdates the Yung-lo emperor. At 56 lb it is one of the largest Chinese jades in western collections.

▼ **26** *Kuang*, bronze, L 209mm, Chinese, transitional style between Shang and Chou dynasties, late 11th – early 10th century BC. This ritual ewer would have been used in ceremonies addressed to deities and ancestors. Its exact purpose is uncertain, but the provision of a ladle (which projects as a tail) and a pouring spout, and the division into two compartments, imply a ritual mixing of two liquids. The bovine head, with horns capped, probably imitates an ox prepared for sacrifice. The body decoration includes dragon-like symmetrical ornament, probably to avert evil spirits, and cicadas, whose emergence from the chrysalis seems intended as a metaphor of ancestral transmigration from physical to spirit world. The bronze carries an inscription, translated by Professor William Watson as 'Shou Kung made this sacred vessel for Father Hsin, may it be preserved for ever.' The green patina is the result of long burial.

◄27 *Page from a Gospel Book*, vellum, 270×190mm, Breton, 9th–10th centuries. This is the most elaborate of a well-known group of manuscripts written and illuminated in Brittany during the late 9th and early 10th centuries. It came to England at some time in the 10th century; it has been glossed in Latin by an English hand of that date. There are also slightly later Anglo-Saxon annotations in two hands. The decoration is the work of one artist who used a crude but vigorous style, with much inventive detail in the miniatures, blending features drawn from earlier, more sophisticated manuscripts. This miniature (fol. 63v) shows St Mark pointing to a book which stands on a curious foliate lectern; above it hovers his symbol, a winged lion.

►28 *An Archbishop or Pope Blessing*, ivory, 337× 114mm, Carolingian or Ottonian, probably 9th century. One of a pair of magnificent ivories made for the cover of a missal. The companion piece, which shows the same ecclesiastic saying mass, is in Frankfurt. The panels probably became separated in the Middle Ages. Above the archbishop or pope stand five servers or deacons. Before him stand seven canons singing with their hands extended: this is one of the earliest known representations of choral accompaniment to a Christian service. The whole scene is enclosed in a border of acanthus leaves. The open book is inscribed with the beginning of Psalm XXIV in the Vulgate, 'Ad te levavi animam meam, deus meus' ('Unto thee, O Lord, do I lift up my soul'), the Introit of the Mass for the first Sunday in Advent. Panels such as this are derived from Byzantine ivory consular diptychs, narrow panels showing the consul in performance of his duties, which he gave as presents to the Emperor, the Senate and influential friends at the beginning of his consulate. This use of classical models is typical of Carolingian art (8th–9th centuries) and reflects Charlemagne's attempts to revive the Roman Empire within his kingdom.

▶ **30** *Page from the Grey-FitzPayn Book of Hours*, vellum, 247 × 167mm, English, *c*1300. The Museum's large collection of medieval illuminated manuscripts is rich in Books of Hours, many of them bequeathed by the Founder, who in his later years devoted much of his wealth to the collection of manuscripts. This magnificent volume is a later addition, bought from William Morris in 1895. Books of Hours are prayer books for the laity; they were originally accretions to the Breviary but by the mid 13th century were made up separately. They contain a calendar of church festivals and saints' days, and suitable prayers for different occasions and each period of the day. The Grey-FitzPayn Hours was probably written and illuminated for the marriage of Sir Richard de Grey of Codnor Castle, Derbyshire, to Joan, daughter of Sir Robert FitzPayn, in 1300/1. This page (fol. 29) shows a large initial D ('Domine labia mea aperies', 'Lord, open thou my lips') in which Christ is depicted blessing Joan FitzPayn. The heraldry includes the arms of Grey of Codnor, Clifford of Frampton (differenced by FitzPayn), and Simon Crey. The artist's delight in the varied forms and behaviour of animals evidently did not inhibit his pleasure in showing them being hunted. This is one of a group of manuscripts illuminated in the same workshop in the Nottingham area.

▲ **29** *The Annunciation*, gold, enamelled *en ronde bosse*, L 67mm, probably Parisian, *c*1400. This exquisite miniature sculpture was probably the central element in an important piece, perhaps a reliquary, made in Paris for the Burgundian court. Its early history is unknown. By the 1860s it was one of the objects in the Geistlicher Schatzkammer (Spiritual Treasury) of the Holy Roman Empire in Vienna. At some time between 1865 and 1875 a number of items, this Annunciation included, were entrusted to an antique dealer, Solomon Weininger, for repair.

The wily Weininger made copies of the originals which were returned, unrecognised, to the Treasury. The originals he sold to wealthy collectors who particularly coveted such treasures of the Middle Ages. *The Annunciation* passed to the Cunliffe collection, which was bequeathed to the Fitzwilliam in 1938. Weininger attempted to work the same trick on the Estenische Kunstsammlung, Vienna. This time the counterfeit was detected, and Weininger died in the Austrian State Prison in 1879, three years after being sentenced for fraud.

Domine labia mea a
peries et os me
um annunti
abit laudem
tuam Deus
in adiutoriu
meum intende Domine ad adiuuā
me festina Gloria patri et filio ꞇ spū
sco Sicut erat in principio et nūc et
semp et in secula seculorum amen·
Deum uerum unum in trinitate et trinitatē
in unitate uenite adoremus·
Uenite exultemus domino iubile
mus deo salutari nro preocupem̄
faciem eius in confessione et in psalmis
iubilemus ei Deum uerum unum intrini
tate et trinitatem in unitate· uenite adoremus·
Quoniam deus magnus dominus ꞇ

◄ **31** Simone Martini (*c*1284–1344): *St Geminianus*, tempera on panel, 59.7×35.8cm, one panel from *St Geminianus, St Augustine and St Michael, each with an angel above.* Part of a polyptych, an altarpiece of several panels, in this case probably five, of which three are in the Fitzwilliam. Two others have been associated with them, a *Virgin and Child* in Frankfurt and a *St Catharine* in a private collection in Italy. The polyptych was painted with the assistance of Simone's workshop, but the outstanding quality of the St Geminianus and St Augustine panels indicates that they are from his own hand. Simone was the most important follower of Duccio in Siena. From him he developed a style based on exquisite linear rhythms and rich and sophisticated colours. Later he worked for the papal court at Avignon and was much influenced by French gothic art. His best-known works are the *Annunciation* in the Uffizi and the fresco cycle of the life of St Martin in Assisi. The presence of St Geminianus and St Augustine in this altarpiece implies that it was painted for an Augustinian convent in San Giminiano, central Italy, whose patron saint was St Geminianus. It has been dated to the 1320s.

▲ **32** Domenico Veneziano (*d*1461): *The Annunciation*, tempera on poplar panel, 27.3×54.0cm. Domenico was one of the most important artists in Florence during the 15th century but very few of his paintings survive. This is the largest of the five predella panels from a signed work, the St Lucy altarpiece, painted at some time between 1442 and 1448 for the Florentine church of S. Lucia dei Magnoli and now in the Uffizi (predella panels, small paintings enframed beneath an altarpiece, usually illustrate scenes from the lives of the saints who appear in the main painting). The St Lucy altarpiece shows *The Virgin and Child enthroned between Sts Lucy, Zenobius, Francis and John the Baptist. The Annunciation* has Domenico Veneziano's characteristic delicate colours and mathematically exact treatment of perspective. The walled garden and its bolted door are traditionally images of the Immaculate Conception, drawn from the description of the beloved as 'a garden enclosed' in the *Song of Songs* IV.12. The use of perspective creates a feeling of serene balance and fulfilment. Close examination reveals the incised perspective lines below the paint, converging on a pin-prick, the vanishing point, on the bolted door – the central symbol of the painting's subject. The Fitzwilliam owns another predella from the same altarpiece, *The Miracle of St Zenobius*, like *The Annunciation* very well preserved.

▲ **33** Antonio Allegri, da Correggio (c1489–1534): *The Nativity*, pen and brown ink, brown wash over red chalk, heightened with white, 243×209mm. Correggio worked for most of his life in Parma, N Italy. His drawings are remarkable for their soft and subtle gradation of tone, and of all the sheets that survive this is the most tender. It is an early study for the painting *The Adoration of the Shepherds ('La Notte')*, commissioned in 1522 for the Pratoneri chapel in the church of S. Prospero in Reggio, 25 km from Parma. Correggio reversed the composition in the finished painting, now in Dresden, and changed many details, especially in the architecture.

▶ **34** Bernardino Pintoricchio (c1454–1513): *Virgin and Child with St John the Baptist*, tempera on panel, 56.7×40.7cm. Pintoricchio was, like Raphael, a pupil of Perugino, from whom he derived his characteristic charmingly pretty idiom. This painting, in superb condition, is very typical of his work, especially in its glowing, fairy-tale landscape and rich colouring. There has been much argument about its date; it was probably painted c1500 and is clearly one of the works that influenced Raphael's *Colonna* altarpiece (c1502), now in the Metropolitan Museum, New York. A very similar *Virgin and Child* by Pintoricchio is in the Ashmolean Museum, Oxford.

▼ **36** Andrea Briosco, called Riccio (1470/5–1532): *Head of a Ram*, bronze, H 110mm. Riccio was the most famous sculptor of the Italian Renaissance to specialise in small bronzes. He was born and worked in Padua; there he trained as a sculptor and also as a goldsmith, which explains the exceptionally delicate handling he brought to his bronzes. His masterpiece is the large Paschal candlestick in the Santo, Padua, but he is most famous for his small bronzes of satyrs and other bucolic subjects whose classical influences reflect the taste of his patrons, the humanist scholars gathered at Padua University. This vividly detailed ram's head is a mount from a candelabrum and dates from the early 1500s.

▲ **35** *Parade Helmet*, cold-chiselled steel, 319×208mm, Milanese, *c*1545–50. The superlative quality of this sumptuous helmet indicates that it was made by the brothers Negroli of Milan, the most famous armourer-artists of the 16th century, who were renowned for elaborately embossed parade armour. This example, like much of their work, is damascened with gold. It may have been made for the Imperial Archduke Ferdinand of the Tyrol, who is known to have been one of their patrons. One side is embossed with a female half-figure blowing a trumpet, representing Fame; on the other, Victory is shown holding a laurel wreath. An open book above Fame is inscribed in Greek 'Thou walkest proudly before the stars'. The visor is a lion mask; the chin pieces are missing. Thought to have been brought to England early in the 19th century, the helmet came to light in 1937 at a sale of theatrical properties.

a   *b*   *c*   *d*   *e*   *f*

▲ **37** *Medieval and Renaissance Coins.*
For over 500 years the dominant
coin of western Christendom was
the silver penny, first coined in the
7th century. In Britain it was first
struck in quantity by Offa of
Mercia in a series remarkable for
its attempt at true portraiture [*a*].
In Germany during the later
Middle Ages a distinctively thin
penny was produced, the
'bracteate', a piece of silver foil
impressed on one side only.
Broader than standard pennies,
bracteates often exhibit elaborate
designs, as in the armature and
vestments of [*c*]. After a lapse of
many centuries, regular gold
coinage was resumed in the 13th
century, first in Italy and later in
France. The Anglo-Gallic series,
struck by the English Crown for its
French possessions, includes some
spectacular examples of gothic art
in coinage. The 'pavillon' of

Edward the Black Prince [*b*], so
called from the canopy he sits
under, mimics the French coinage
of Philip VI.

The Italian Renaissance was a
golden age of coin portraiture. The
lead was given by the Sforza court
at Milan [*d*]. In Germany,
meanwhile, improved methods of
silver extraction made it possible
to produce large silver pieces, later
known as talers. The most notable
were those of the Austrian
Hapsburgs, e.g. the early portrait
'taler' of Emperor Maximilian I
[*e*]. The reverse type of the
Scottish eighty-shilling piece of
James VI is a remarkable
exception to the dull heraldic or
armorial types of most European
issues: a Scottish lion with sword,
below a cloud inscribed with the
name of Jehovah and the legend TE
SOLUM VEREOR, 'Thee alone do I
fear' [*f*].

[*a*] Britain, Mercia, Eadhun for
Offa (757–96), Canterbury, *c*787–
92, silver penny: bust of Offa/
lozenge; [*b*] France, Guyenne,
Edward the Black Prince (1362–
72), Poitiers, gold 'pavillon':
Edward enthroned/ornamental
quatrefoil; [*c*] Germany,
Brandenburg, Albert the Bear
(1134–70), Ballenstedt, silver
penny ('bracteate'): Albert with
his wife, Sophia; [*d*] Italy, Milan,
Gian Galeazzo Maria Sforza
(1476–94), 1481, gold double
ducat: bust of Gian Galeazzo
Maria/shield of arms; [*e*] Austria,
Maximilian I (1493–1519), Hall,
silver *Kaiserguldiner*: bust of
Maximilian/shields of arms; [*f*]
Scotland, James VI (1567–1625),
Edinburgh, 1591, gold eighty
shillings ('hat-piece'): bust of
James/lion; above, cloud with
name of Jehovah in Hebrew.

◄ **38** *Dish*, maiolica, D 463mm, Italian, Cafaggiolo, *c*1510–20. Tin-glazed earthenware (maiolica) was made in many centres in Italy during the Renaissance. This spectacular dish, a highlight of the Museum's extensive collection, comes from Tuscany. The full significance of the scene in the middle has yet to be explained; it may represent a power-struggle between two families or factions. The inscription E COSI VA CHE TROPO VOLLE means roughly 'This is what happens to him who wants too much'. The rest of the decoration is of classical derivation and would have appealed greatly to a highly educated patron. On the base of the dish is a battle between centaurs and satyrs, and on the rim, 'cameo' medallions and grotesques. The subjects of the medallions, drawn from the Bible and Roman history, include David and Goliath, Mucius Scaevola, Judith with the head of Holofernes and the death of Dido. On the back is a trophy composed of two quivers, an arrow and a bow, surrounded by foliage on delicate coiling stems and a border of striped petals. Maiolica dishes frequently had some decoration on their backs, but rarely so carefully painted as this.

▼ **39** *Tazza*, glass, enamelled and gilt, D 288mm, Venetian, *c*1500. In the 14th century the glass manufactories of Venice became the finest in Europe, and throughout the following two centuries produced glassware of unrivalled quality. Enamelled vessels were a speciality; this example, a footed tray, has the winged lion of St Mark, the emblem of Venice, in the centre.

◄40 Quentin Metsys (1464/5–1530): *Erasmus*, cast bell metal, 1519. Metsys, one of the most important artists to convey the ideas of the Italian Renaissance to N Europe, portrayed his friend Erasmus twice: in a famous painting and on his only recorded portrait medal, of which this is an unsurpassed example. The head is inscribed IMAGO AD VIVA(M) EFFIGIE(M) EXPRESSA, 'This is his image taken from life', and, in Greek, 'his writings will exhibit it better': the medal depicts Erasmus' outer form but for his spiritual essence the spectator must study his works. ER and ROT by the head stand for 'Erasmus of Rotterdam'. The reverse bears Erasmus' device, a terminal figure inscribed TERMINUS, and three mottoes: 'I yield to none', 'Death is the goal of all things', and 'Keep in sight the end of a long life'. Desiderius Erasmus (*c*1466–1536) spent most of his life in Rotterdam; his writings and biblical scholarship were influential throughout Europe. Between 1511 and 1514 he was in Cambridge, at Queens' College, attempting to work despite his dislike of the climate and the college ale.

►41 Joos van Cleve (*c*1485–1540/1): *Virgin and Child*, oil on panel, 61.0×45.1cm, probably *c*1525–30. Van Cleve spent most of his life in Antwerp, apart from a period of travel perhaps in Italy and certainly to the court of François I, where he painted portraits of the French royal family. This is one of the finest examples of his tender realism and shows the influence of both Italian painters and, in the exquisite landscape, the Flemish tradition.

43

42 *Basin*, silver-gilt with embossed and chased decoration, D 457mm, French, Paris, 1560–1, maker's mark indecipherable. In the 16th century magnificent displays of plate were arranged on sidetables at banquets to impress the guests. Fanciful standing cups (e.g. **49**) and ornate ewers and basins were intended for this purpose, rather than for use at table. Intricate embossed and chased marine ornament, inspired by classical mythology, was a characteristic feature of silver influenced by the Italian Mannerist style. It appealed greatly to contemporary patrons, who delighted in sophisticated decoration displaying the goldsmith's technical virtuosity. The strapwork on the boss of this basin and the tritons, nereids and other sea creatures around it were derived from engravings by Jacques Androuet de Cerceau, the most influential French designer of the mid 16th century. The coat of arms of Featherstonhaugh in the centre is an early-19th-century insertion.

43 *Adoration of the Magi*, alabaster carved in high relief and parcel gilt, 785×685×200mm, probably Flemish, *c*1540. The carving is signed with the initials AH, as yet unidentified. The original location and the circumstances of commission are unknown, but the unusually prominent star and the rosary in Joseph's hand probably indicate a Dominican origin. The handling of the angelic choir and the architectural details show that the artist was acquainted with Italian work. Northern influence, perhaps received through Dürer, is evident in the flamboyant costumes and accessories of the Magi. But the only known parallel to the composition is a much simpler small Spanish wood-carving of about the same date. The carving is so handled that a low view-point is best, and the construction at the back shows that at some stage the piece was built into a wall. Restoration and cleaning revealed that the head of the Virgin is neither the original one, nor a specially made replacement; possibly the relief was damaged in the wave of Protestant iconoclasm which swept the Low Countries in the 1560s.

◄ 44 Paolo Veronese (*c*1528–88): *Hermes, Herse and Aglauros*, oil on canvas, 232.4×173.0cm. This splendid late example of Veronese's sensuous and festive art was painted soon after 1576, probably for Rudolph II, Emperor of Austria. The subject, rare in art (though the Museum has a maiolica plate from Gubbio, dated 1522, which also depicts it), is taken from Ovid's *Metamorphoses*, II. Hermes bribed Aglauros to give him access to her sister Herse, whom he loved. Athena made Aglauros jealous of Herse as punishment for having earlier disobeyed her, and here Hermes, striding into Herse's bedroom, turns Aglauros to stone as she attempts to bar his way. The scene is characterised by Veronese's love of luxurious settings and costumes and masterly sense of colour. Fashionable Palladian architecture forms a backdrop to the glamorous figure of Herse, who is lightly dressed in expensive fabrics (her blue shawl, complementing the sky, provides the dominant tone). On the table is a viol and Herse's hand rests on an open score, beside an exquisitely depicted glass vase of flowers. Aglauros writhes in a superbly complex pose around Hermes' advancing leg, one hand pressed on his foot, the other

pushing him away. This picture was once in the collection of Queen Christina of Sweden; after her death in Rome it passed, with **45** and **46**, into the d'Orléans collection. When this was auctioned after the French Revolution Lord Fitzwilliam purchased all three – the pride of his collection and of the Museum he founded.

▲ 45 Palma Vecchio (*c*1480–1528): *Venus and Cupid*, oil on canvas, 118.1×208.9cm, *c*1520/5. Palma Vecchio, a Venetian, was probably trained by Bellini. This is one of his finest works, and provides a splendid example of the voluptuous blondes for which he was famous (very much a Venetian taste: compare Veronese's Herse (**44**) and Titian's Venus (**46**)). Among his several versions of Venus reclining in a landscape this is unusual in its inclusion of Cupid. There has been some argument as to whether Cupid is taking or giving the arrow; probably the former, for that seems the most natural interpretation of his posture, and Venus is more likely to be providing than receiving the weapon with which he will wreak havoc.

▲ **46** Tiziano Vecelli, called Titian (*c*1490–1576): *Venus and Cupid with a Luteplayer*, oil on canvas, 150.5×196.8cm. This is one of a series of nude Venuses with musicians: here and in the Metropolitan Museum, New York, a lutenist, in the others, an organist. A madrigal has been played; the bass part lies open in front of Venus on top of a closed tenor part, the recorder droops in her hand and the viola da gamba is propped against her couch. The painting may be an allegory of the hierarchy of the senses, representing sensuality sublimated through music and visual beauty, or a celebration of consummated love, a pendant to the organist scenes showing love's arousal. Turner warmly praised the effect of the landscape: 'Brilliant, clear and with deep-toned shadow, it makes up the equilibrium of the whole by contrasting its variety with the pulpy softness of the female figure, glowing with all the charms of colour . . . rich and swelling.'

►**47** Tiziano Vecelli, called Titian (*c*1490–1576): *Tarquin and Lucretia*, oil on canvas, 188.9×145.1cm. Sextus Tarquin, son of the last king of Rome, Tarquinius Superbus (who reigned, according to tradition, 534–510 BC), compelled Lucretia, the virtuous wife of his kinsman and a noted beauty, to submit to his lust by threatening to kill her and make the act appear a retribution for adultery with a slave. The next day Lucretia told her father and husband what had happened and then stabbed herself; Tarquin was forced to flee Rome. This masterpiece was delivered in 1571 to Philip II of Spain, one of Titian's most important patrons of that period, for whom he supplied numerous mythological paintings, usually erotic. Titian was over 80 when he completed this canvas: it shows unflagging powers of invention and extraordinary vitality. Its disturbing violence is in sharp contrast with the easy sensuality of his *Venus and Cupid with a Luteplayer*.

◄ 48 Hans Eworth (active 1540–74): *Unknown Lady*, oil on panel, 109.9×80.0cm. Hans Eworth came from Antwerp and worked in London from the late 1540s to 1574; he has been identified with the court painter to Mary I who signed his works HE. The sitter for this splendid and sensitive portrait has the direct but guarded look characteristic of Eworth's work; there has been much argument about her identity. The picture was for long called *Mary I when Princess*. The costume allows the picture to be dated *c*1550–5, and Mary came to the throne in 1553; however, if she was the sitter the artist has flattered her, both by softening her features and by showing her as a young woman – Mary was born in 1516 and would therefore have been about 35 to 40 by this time. The sitter's rings imply that she is unmarried, and the large jewel on her chest shows Esther kneeling before her husband King Ahasuerus, who stretches out his sceptre to her (*Esther* V.2) – an incident regarded by theologians of the day as a 'type' (prefiguration) of the Virgin Mary's coronation as Queen of Heaven. This may refer to Mary's position as heir to the throne and the hope for a Catholic revival to follow the Protestant zenith of Edward VI's reign, or it may simply indicate that the sitter's name was Mary.

▲ 49 *Nautilus Cup*, shell with engraved decoration, mounted in silver-gilt, H 238mm, English, London, 1585–6, maker's mark TR in monogram. The 16th-century voyages of discovery opened up the Indian Ocean and Far East to European trade. As a result, exotic natural materials and costly manufactured goods such as porcelain reached the west in greater quantities than before. Rare shells, coconuts, ostrich eggs and eastern ceramics were especially prized and were mounted in precious metals to form ornate cups which their owners displayed at meals, gave away to honoured guests, or kept in private treasuries (see also **52**). This is one of the finest English examples to have survived. The shell forming the bowl was decorated in China. The mounts, made in London, are stylistically similar to those of cups made in Flanders, but details such as the floral engraving round the rim are typically English.

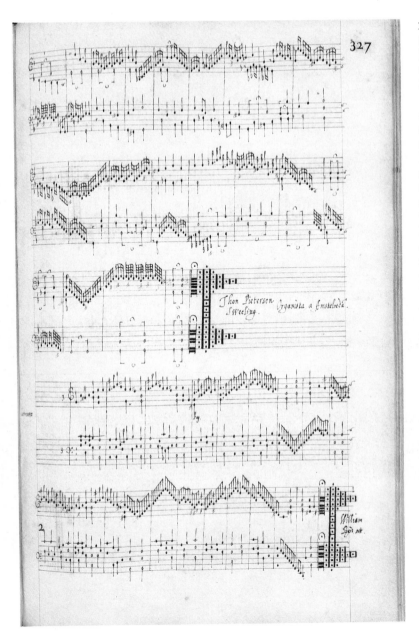

▲ **50** *The Fitzwilliam Virginal Book*, 345×235mm, English, early 17th century. This is the most important contemporary collection of 16th- and 17th-century keyboard music in existence. It contains nearly 300 works for keyboard instruments by some 30 of the greatest composers of the time. They were copied out by Francis Tregian the younger, who was convicted as a recusant in 1608/9 and died in the Fleet Prison. The book was bequeathed by the Founder and is the chief treasure of an extensive holding of music manuscripts. On this folio (327) is the conclusion of a Fantasia by the Dutch organist J.P.Sweelinck (1562–1621) and a Coranto by William Byrd (*c*1538–1623).

▶ **51** Tudor and Stuart examples from the Museum's extensive collection of portrait miniatures (16th to 20th centuries). [*a*] Lucas Horenbout (*c*1490/5–1544): *Henry VIII*, body colour on vellum on card, 53×48mm. The earliest miniature in the collection and one of the first painted in England. Horenbout, of a Ghent family of manuscript illuminators, worked at the English court 1525–40. The decorative borders incorporating the initials of Henry and Katharine of Aragon show the connection between manuscript illumination and early portrait miniatures. [*c* and *d*] Nicholas Hilliard (*c*1547–1619): *Queen Elizabeth*, 58×45mm, and *Henry Wriothesley, 3rd Earl of Southampton*, 41×32mm, both body colour on vellum on card. The detail and precision of his miniatures reflect Hilliard's early training as a goldsmith. The queen's portrait is one of several by him; that of Southampton is the earliest known of Shakespeare's patron. [*b*] Isaac Oliver (*d*1617): *Henry, Prince of Wales*, water colour on vellum on card, 53×40mm. Oliver, Hilliard's pupil and later his chief rival, prospered at the court of James I, where Flemish realism was superseding Elizabethan jewelled abstraction. This portrait of James' eldest son (1594–1612) suggests a Roman cameo. [*f*] John Hoskins (*d*1665): *Algernon Sidney(?)*, watercolour on vellum on card, 64×51mm. A late work by Hoskins showing Van Dyck's influence on contemporary portraiture. Sidney (1622–83) was a political theorist, executed for involvement in the republican Rye House Plot. [*e*] Samuel Cooper (1609–72): *Lady Margaret Leigh (Ley)*, watercolour on vellum on card, 70×55mm. Cooper was Hoskins' nephew and pupil and the most successful (and expensive) miniaturist of his day.

a

c d

f

▶ **53** *Hawk*, composite body, alkaline glazed and copper lustred, H 464mm, Iran, late 12th–13th centuries. The white bodies of near-eastern fine wares produced from the 13th century onwards consist of a mixture of powdered quartz, white clay and potash described in a manuscript of 1301 by Abū'l-Qāsim, a potter from Kashan. It was most probably developed to emulate the white wares of China, but was related to the so-called 'faience' or frit of ancient Egypt and Mesopotamia. It was covered with a clear alkaline glaze. The decoration on this hawk was done in a second firing: the design was painted in copper salts and gently burnished after the firing. The function of the piece seems to have been purely decorative, although the bird itself and the cartouches of men and women on horseback and of birds indicate that it was made to celebrate the distinctively aristocratic sport of falconry.

▲ **52** *Isnik Jug mounted in silver-gilt*, H 254mm, the jug Turkish (Isnik), 16th century, the mounts English, London, maker's mark IH, hallmark for 1592. The jug, decorated underglaze in red, blue, turquoise, green and black, was probably imported into England soon after it was made. The mounts have a practical purpose in that they cover the rims, which are especially prone to chipping, but they serve primarily to aggrandise an exotic product. (For another example of a foreign vessel in an Elizabethan mount see **49**.)

◄ **54** *Mosque Lamp*, glass with enamelled decoration, H 353mm, Syrian, Damascus, *c*1350. Mosque lamps are in fact not lamps but ornamental shades for oil lamps placed inside them. The form was developed in the late 13th century; most of the finest examples, such as this, were made in Syria in the 14th and 15th centuries. The yellowish-green glass and enamelled decoration are typical. The six glass loops are for attaching the thin chains by which the lamp was suspended. There are two bold kufic inscriptions, one from the Koran (Sura XXIV.35), the other ascribing the lamp to the munificence of Emir Saichu, whose heraldic device, a cup, also appears in the decoration. He was a slave who rose to become cup-bearer and later chief minister to one of the Mameluke sultans of Egypt. In 1355, two years before his assassination, he built a cloister and mausoleum in Cairo. It was to light one of these that this lamp, a masterpiece of medieval glass-making and enamelling, was made.

► **55** Riza-i'Abbasi (active 161⟨ 40): *Bagpipe Player*, point of the brush, ink, watercolour and body colour with gold, 178×104mm. Riza-i'Abbasi, who worked in Isfahan, was the foremost Persian painter of his day. He was renowned for the great beauty of his calligraphic line and delicate use of wash – qualities which this miniature painting (dated 1033 AH, i.e. AD1624) superbly demonstrates.

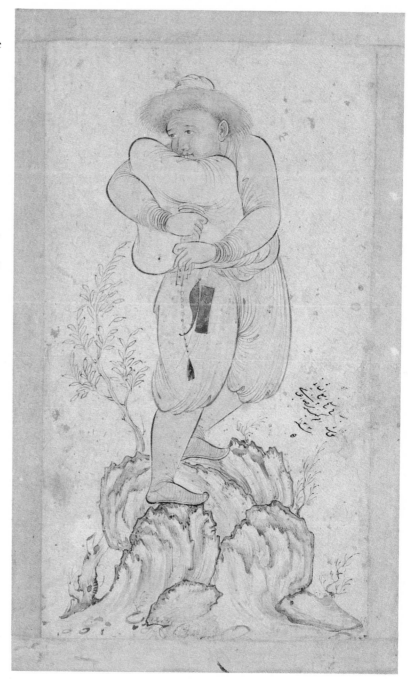

◄ **56** Sir Peter Paul Rubens (1577–1640): *Head of a Bearded Man*, oil on oak panel, 68.6×53.3cm. This imposing study was used for the head of Caspar in *The Adoration of the Magi*, the central panel of a triptych commissioned for the church of St Jean, Malines, in 1616. Rubens made such studies from the life and kept them in his studio as part of his stock-in-trade. This head was probably included in a group of studies from life by Rubens or Van Dyck which was sold at the disposal of Rubens' effects after his death, in 1640.

▲ **57** Sir Peter Paul Rubens (1577–1640): *The Death of Hippolytus*, oil on copper, 50.2×70.8cm. Hippolytus repelled the advances of his stepmother, Phaedra, and in revenge she accused him of attempting to rape her. Theseus, his father, in fury cursed Hippolytus, who was thereupon killed while driving his chariot along the shore by a bull sent by Theseus' father, Poseidon, god of the sea. This spectacular cabinet-sized painting, which has been dated *c*1611, exhibits Rubens' genius for creating drama with vigorous action and forceful and sensuous colour. The sprawling figure of Hippolytus was used by Rubens in several compositions; it is based on a life study inspired by a presentation drawing by Michelangelo now at Windsor. A sketchier version of this picture, without the fleeing figures in the rear (they are derived from Annibale Carracci's *Polyphemus*, in the Palazzo Farnese, Rome) and the shells and sea creatures in the foreground, is in the Princes Gate Collection, bequeathed to the Courtauld Institute, London.

◄**58** Sir Anthony van Dyck (1599–1641): *Virgin and
Child*, oil on panel, 146.7×109.2cm. The Fitzwilliam
is one of the few British public collections to own a
devotional work by Van Dyck, an artist best known in
this country for his portraits (fine examples of which
are also in the Museum). This picture was painted
soon after Van Dyck's return home to Antwerp from
Italy in 1628 and before his departure in 1631 for
England, where he had his greatest successes at the
court of Charles I. It displays a fusion of the influence
of Rubens, whose chief assistant he had been, with an
appreciation of the Italian painters, Titian, Guido
Reni and Raphael, whose work he had seen on his
travels. His Italian sketchbook (British Museum)
contains many related copies of Virgin and Child
compositions. This important painting was imported
into England in 1790 and subsequently acquired by
Francis, 3rd Earl of Bridgewater. His descendant sent
it to auction in 1976; it was subsequently acquired for
the Museum by public appeal.

▲ **59** Sir Anthony van Dyck (1599–1641): (left) *Lucas
Vorsterman*, black chalk, 244×179mm, (right) *Lucas
Vorsterman*, etching, 244×157mm. In 1636 Van Dyck
had a great European success with the publication of
a collection of 80 prints by various artists after his
drawings and grisailles, the *Iconographie*, which aimed
to circulate the portraits of eminent men of the time.
A second, extended, version appeared posthumously
in 1645. Van Dyck himself etched only about 20 of his
designs, including his self-portrait, and this portrait
which is perhaps his masterpiece in etching. Lucas
Vorsterman (1595–1675) was a famous engraver who
produced several plates for the *Iconographie*. The
preliminary drawing (left) may have been made by
Van Dyck in 1631 in Antwerp, where he stood
godfather to Vorsterman's daughter Antonia on
10 May. The proof of the etching reproduced here
(right) is a brilliant specimen of its first state, before
the addition of lettering.

▲ **60** Rembrandt van Rijn (1606–69): *Jacob Shown the Bloodstained Coat of Joseph*, pen, brown ink and brown wash, corrections in body colour, 164×221mm. This drawing illustrates *Genesis* XXXVII.32–4. Jacob is on his knees; behind him an old woman, possibly Leah, raises her arms; one of Joseph's brothers stoops towards Jacob; another holds the stained coat and a third leans on his shepherd's crook. With rapid and expressive calligraphy Rembrandt has created a scene of deep pathos. His alterations to the head of the left-hand brother have become transparent, revealing its original position. Rembrandt also treated this subject in an early etching and two other drawings; this drawing can be dated *c*1654/5.

▶ **61** Johann Liss (*c*1597–1629/30): *A Bacchanalian Feast*, oil on panel, 34.2×27.3cm. Liss received his earliest education as a painter in the artistic obscurity of N Germany. He trained himself further in Antwerp and perhaps Paris, moving to Italy in 1621. The community of northern painters in Rome nicknamed him 'Pan', which admirably suits this sensuous picture of *c*1617 – one of the very rare works Liss painted before he left for Italy, and his only painting in a British public collection outside London. The influence of the contemporary work of Jacob Jordaens on the figures is very strong. Changes to the landscape during the course of painting – the foliage has been reduced to show more sky – suggest that Liss was shifting his attention from the older German traditions of landscape painting towards the newer fashion of Adam Elsheimer, whose work greatly affected Rubens and younger artists of the day, including Claude (see **69**).

64

◄ 62 Frans Hals (1581/5–1666): *Portrait of a Man*, oil on canvas, 80×67cm. One of Hals' bravura portraits, painted with even greater panache than his brilliant, much earlier, *'Laughing Cavalier'*. The almost monochromatic effect of the restrained palette is as characteristic of his last years as the bold and fluid brushwork. Hals' technique, carefully contrived (despite its apparent total spontaneity) to capture fleeting emotions, gestures and expressions was much admired by Manet. When the painting entered the Museum in 1879 the sitter's hat and the background had been painted out in brown, probably in the late 18th or early 19th century, in an effort to make the subject appear more respectable.

▲ 63 Jacques Fouquier (1590/1–1659): *Winter Scene*, oil on panel, 57.8×76.8cm. Fouquier, a Flemish painter, is said to have trained under Jan I (Velvet) Brueghel and Joos de Momper and worked briefly with Rubens, painting landscape backgrounds for which Rubens provided the figures. From 1621 he spent much of his time in France; he was commissioned by Louis XIII to provide paintings for the Louvre but resigned after quarrelling with Poussin. *Winter Scene* is Fouquier's earliest known dated landscape (1617) and the only painting by him in an English public collection. The centrally placed tree occurs in many of his compositions.

◄ **64** Aelbert Cuyp (1620–91): *Sunset after Rain*, oil on panel, 83.9×69.9cm. Cuyp, a Dutch painter of landscapes, still-lifes, animals, portraits and sea pieces, is best known for his pictures of cattle in landscapes depicted with poetic sensitivity to light and atmosphere. This is a very beautiful example, which has been dated 1648–52; its shape appears to be unique in Cuyp's work, indicating that it was executed for a specific oval opening in panelling. Most of Cuyp's paintings came to Britain, and greatly influenced the English landscape tradition; this one was in England as early as the 18th century and was copied by Gainsborough. Its evocative title dates from the 19th century.

▲ **65** Salomon van Ruysdael (1600/3–70): *Farm Buildings in a Landscape*, oil on panel, 30.2×47.0cm. Salomon van Ruysdael was one of the leading Dutch landscape artists of the mid 17th century. This painting, in excellent condition, is dated either 1626 or 1628 (the last digit is unclear); like all his early works it is of refreshing simplicity. Salomon was the father of the landscape painter Jacob Salomonsz. van Ruysdael and uncle of Jacob van Ruisdael, the family's best-known painter, of whose landscapes the Fitzwilliam owns four.

▲ **66** *Scenes from the Story of David and Bathsheba,* stumpwork, satin worked in linen, silk and metal threads, purl, seed pearls, ostrich feathers and talc, 460×575mm, English, dated 1700. Stumpwork is needlework in which all or most of the ornament is raised into relief on a foundation of wool or wood. (Purl is a cord of twisted gold or silver wire, used as bordering; talc is a piece of transparent mica.) This spectacularly elaborate panel exploits most of the materials and techniques of the 17th- and 18th-century needlewoman. It illustrates *2 Samuel* XI: (top left) King David on his roof watches (centre) Bathsheba bathing; (top right) Bathsheba's husband, Uriah, is killed in battle; (bottom left) David in his tent (note the royal coat of arms) is brought news of Uriah's death; (bottom right) Bathsheba is brought to David. The Fitzwilliam's collection of textiles includes the largest number of English samplers in any British public collection.

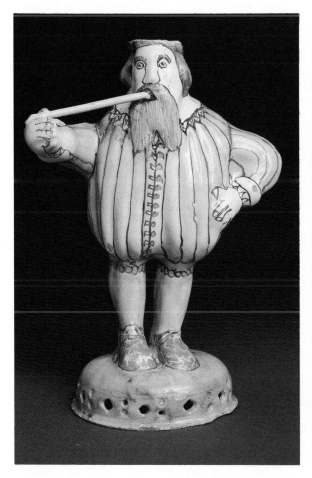

▲ **67** *Nobody*, tin-glazed earthenware, H 230mm, English, London, initialled R^M M, dated 1675. This pipe-smoking figure, one of the most unusual pieces of English delftware in the Fitzwilliam's extensive collection of English ceramics, represents that unassuming character who is blamed for so many human failings and misdeeds. He was well known in 16th-century Germany as *Niemand*, a scapegoat for the carelessness of servants, and often depicted amidst broken pots and pans. In England, by a visual pun, he came to be envisaged as a body-less man, whose head and arms grew straight out of voluminous breeches – his guise on the frontispiece of a popular play, *Nobody and Somebody*, c1606. By 1675 fashions had changed, but the image persisted. Although this figure is hollow and may have had a hat-shaped cover, it is doubtful if it was meant to be functional. The initials on the base are probably its owners'.

▲ **68** Frans Greenwood (1680–1762): *Goblet*, stipple-engraved glass, H 249mm. Greenwood was born in Rotterdam of English parents and spent his life in Holland, first as a merchant and later as a civil servant. In his spare time he was a poet, a painter of miniatures and an engraver of glasses. His scenes on glasses were usually copied from prints, and it was probably the example of mezzotints or dotted engravings that led him to make the innovation of stippling the design with his diamond point rather than engraving lines. His glasses were all produced between 1720 and 1749; this splendid example probably dates from the 1730s. The glass itself is most likely English. The design is after Antonio Tempesta (1555–1630), an Italian painter and engraver, who etched numerous scenes of riding and hunting.

69

▼ **69** Claude Lorrain (1600–82): *Pastoral Landscape with a View of Lake Albano and Castel Gandolfo*, oil on metal, 30.5×37.5cm. A small and glowing example of Claude's Italian landscapes. The poetic light and balanced composition of his paintings brought him an immense reputation, and he was regarded as a model for all landscape artists for more than a century after his death. This picture is one of a pair painted *c*1639 for Pope Urban VIII (*d*1644); it shows his newly completed summer residence at Castel Gandolfo seen from across Lake Albano. The painting remained in the collection of the pope's family, the Barberini, until 1962. Turner, a lifelong admirer of Claude, saw and sketched it in Italy in 1819.

▲ **70** Sebastien Bourdon (1616–71): *Classical Landscape*, oil on copper, 20.3×31.8cm. Bourdon was a much-travelled artist from Montpellier who worked in Rome, Venice, Paris and, under the patronage of Queen Christina, Sweden. In 1654 he resettled in Paris, where Nicolas Poussin's classical art inspired some of his finest work, including this luminously beautiful small landscape. It demonstrates how he disciplined the flamboyant baroque idiom and Venetian colouring of his early work into cooler tones and more restrained compositions without losing his personal limpid handling of paint.

◄**71** *(attributed to)* John Bushnell (*d*1701): *Charles II*, terracotta, H 785mm. This bust (*c*1678) shows the king aged about 48. Its early history is obscure; it came from the demolished Serjeant's Inn, Chancery Lane, London, and may have belonged to or even have been commissioned by Francis North, 1st Baron Guildford (1637–85), who was Lord Chancellor under Charles II, a patron of the arts and a friend of the king. He paid for the hall of Serjeant's Inn (1669–77) and lived next door. Bushnell was a vain and temperamental sculptor who fled from England to escape matrimonial difficulties and for many years worked in Italy. This bust, if it is by him, was executed after his return. Free-standing busts by 17th-century English artists are rare and are usually the result of continental influence. The liveliness of this work indicates a knowledge of Italian baroque sculpture, that of Bernini in particular. Other works by Bushnell include two tombs in Westminster Abbey and the bust of Mrs Pepys in St Olave's, London.

►**72** Gaspar van den Hoecke (active 1603–41): *Flowers*, oil on wood, 84.5×52.0cm. One of the most important bequests received by the Fitzwilliam is the large collection of flower paintings and drawings formed by Henry Broughton, 2nd Lord Fairhaven. (For an example of a watercolour from the collection, see **87**.) The paintings are mostly Dutch and Flemish works of the 17th and 18th centuries. This is the only known flower piece by van den Hoecke, who is otherwise known as a history painter. Dated 1614, it is clearly inspired by the work of Jan I Brueghel.

◄73 Kitagawa Utamaro (1753–1806): *Episode from the Parody of Chūshingura*, colour woodcut, 386×254mm, Japanese, c1797. Utamaro was a painter and designer of woodcuts who specialised in depicting courtesans going about their daily routines, with every detail of their posture, dress and expression carefully observed. This is the second of a series of 12 scenes which parody episodes in the famous Japanese play *Chūshingura*, or *The History of the 47 Faithful Rōnin*. The Rōnin were warriors who owed allegiance to no lord, and the play recounts their heroic deeds. In Utamaro's mock-heroic version, the roles of the Rōnin are taken by celebrated beauties whose everyday actions travesty the great deeds of the heroes (rather in the manner of Pope's *The Rape of the Lock*). Here two girls, Itsutomi and Muranoya, parody the scene in which Honzō cuts off the branch of a pine tree with Wakasa's sword in Act 2. The album in which the 12 scenes are bound once belonged to Edmond de Goncourt and an autograph note by him, describing the work, is pasted inside the cover.

◄74 *Mei-p'ing*, porcelain, decorated underglaze in cobalt-blue and copper red, H 330mm, Chinese, Ch'ien-lung period (1736–95). *Mei-p'ing* means 'plum vase' and refers to the function of the type: to hold a branch of flowering prunus. The decoration on the main body shows a scholar in a landscape with the 'Three Friends', pine, bamboo and prunus. These symbolise longevity – the pine resin was held to turn to amber after 1000 years of life; loyalty – the bamboo bends under pressure but springs back afterwards; and rejuvenation – the plum blossoms on bare branches when snow is on the ground. All are qualities expected of the *chun-tzu*, the perfect Chinese gentleman. The three are also associated with Taoism, Confucianism and Buddhism, the chief faiths of traditional China. A second landscape is painted on the shoulder of the vase.

▲ **75** Antoine Watteau (1684–1721): *A Man Playing the Flute*, 'en trois crayons', i.e. red, black and white chalk, 170×173mm. Watteau made numerous crayon drawings which he kept in large bound volumes and used as the occasion arose in the composition of his paintings. Characteristically, he made use of this figure more than once – in a *Concert Champêtre* of *c*1707 or *c*1716, and on two other occasions known from prints. The left-hand figure on a sheet of studies in the British Museum shows a flautist full length in the same pose, but with the head only lightly indicated.

▼ 76 *Two-Handled Cup, Cover and Saucer*, soft-paste porcelain decorated with enamel-colours and gilt, H of cup 143mm, D of saucer 218mm, French, Vincennes, 1756, painter's mark of Tabary. Experiments to produce porcelain were initiated in the disused royal château at Vincennes *c*1739–40. By 1745 a satisfactory soft-paste had been achieved and a company was formed to exploit it. In 1753 the king became a major shareholder and the factory assumed the title Manufacture Royale de Porcelaine. Three years later it moved to Sèvres, which was more conveniently situated, between Versailles and Paris. Two-handled cups with covers were known as *gobelets à lait* and this large size may have been the *gobelet à lait chopine* mentioned in the factory's records. It holds an English pint, approximately equivalent to a French *chopine*. This example illustrates to perfection the exquisitely white paste, delicate painting and subtly applied gilding for which Vincennes porcelain was famous. Bird-painting, in colours or in gold, was one of the most characteristic types of decoration executed at Vincennes. On undecorated grounds, as here, it is rare. More often it is found in reserves with ornate gilt frames against a ground of rich dark blue *(bleu lapis)* or turquoise *(bleu celeste)*. The painter's mark on the base is a variant of that used by Tabary, who specialised in bird-painting.

◄**78** *Angry Harlequin*, porcelain, H
187mm, German (Meissen),
*c*1738. The Royal Saxon Porcelain
Manufacture founded by
Augustus the Strong, Elector of
Saxony and King of Poland, in
1710 at Meissen, near Dresden,
was the first European factory that
successfully imitated Chinese
porcelain. Its first director was the
alchemist J.F.Böttger, who
discovered for Europe the secret of
making hard-paste porcelain

(1708). Its artistic supremacy in
its first 50 years was due to the
employment of outstanding
painters and modellers. This
figure is by J.J.Kändler, appointed
Chief Modeller in 1733. It is one of
a series of characters from the
Italian Commedia dell'Arte; its
baroque features – the
exaggerated pose and strong
colours – are typical of the figures
produced at Meissen in the 1730s
and 1740s.

◄ **77** Bernardo Bellotto (1721–80): *Entrance to the Grand Canal, Venice*, oil on canvas, 59.3× 94.9cm. Bellotto was Canaletto's nephew and pupil; his attention to architectural detail and sense of composition are clearly inspired by his uncle's work, though his colours tend to be cooler in tone. Like most of his early work, this painting is quite closely based on one by Canaletto (in a private collection in the USA). In 1746 Bellotto left Venice, never to return. He worked in various parts of N Italy (two views of Florence are in the Fitzwilliam), Dresden, Vienna and Munich before settling in Warsaw, where most of

his paintings remain. This scene was bequeathed to the Museum by the Founder; with his two Canalettos, it forms the nucleus of an attractive group of works by the Venetian *vedutisti* (view painters), who have been consistently popular in England since the 18th century. It shows a view from the Campiello del Traghetto di S. Maria Zobenigo, with S. Maria della Salute on the far side of the canal flanked by the Abbazia and church of S. Gregorio on the right and the Seminario Patriarcale and Dogana on the left. In the distance the Riva degli Schiavoni is visible through the ships' masts.

▼ **79** Francesco Guardi (1712–93): *Forte S. Andrea del Lido, Venice*, oil on canvas, 31.7×52.7mm. Guardi painted mostly views of his native Venice and its lagoon. They were less esteemed in his time than the scrupulously exact pictures of Canaletto and Bellotto but are now highly appreciated, thanks to his interest in capturing transient effects of light and atmosphere, which anticipates the aims of the French Impressionists. His brother Gian-Antonio, with whom he sometimes collaborated, is also represented in the Fitzwilliam. This painting and its pair (also in the Museum) belong to a series of views of the lagoon, all similar in style and size, which form an independent group within Francesco's oeuvre and have been dated to the 1760s.

▲ **80** Thomas Gainsborough (1727–88): *'Heneage Lloyd and His Sister'*, oil on canvas, 64.1× 81.0cm. This is one of several small landscapes with full-length figures that Gainsborough painted early in his career. It shows the artist combining the naturalism of Dutch 17th-century landscape painting with the artifice of the French rococo spirit that he had encountered in London in the work of his master, Hubert Gravelot, who had studied under Boucher. The picture's provenance is uncertain; it is traditionally known as a Lloyd family portrait and may well come from Hintlesham Hall, Suffolk, where the family lived, but the identification of the boy as Heneage Lloyd (1742–76) has been questioned. On stylistic grounds the painting has been dated to the 1750s, a date supported by the costumes – the boy's breeches are buckled above the knee, a fashion of the 1750s, and the girl's cap was fashionable from the 1730s to the 1760s. Heneage Lloyd would have been eight in 1750 and the boy in the picture has been said to look older, but the miniature versions of adult costume in which 18th-century children were dressed make it hard for us to judge his age accurately. Heneage was the second son of Sir Richard Lloyd and became a captain in the Coldstream Guards. The girl has not been identified.

▼ 81 *Watch and Chatelaine*, the watch by William Webster, the outer case by George Michael Moser (1704–83), gold, L 780mm, English, London, 1761–2. Moser, a goldsmith, enameller and medallist born in Schaffhausen, came to England *c*1720. He was a foundation member of the Royal Academy and its first Keeper, and drawing master to George III when Prince; he introduced the art of rococo goldsmithing into England. This delicately chased watchcase shows Mars, Venus and Cupid. The heart-shaped pendant on the chatelaine encloses braided hair and is inscribed TOI SEUL ME FIXE ('I am constant to you alone'). The Museum's collection of watches includes Beethoven's, the younger Pitt's and Gainsborough's.

▲ 82 Louis François Roubiliac (*c*1705–62): *G.F.Handel*, terracotta, H 470mm. The model for the marble statue (now in the Victoria and Albert Museum) commissioned in 1738 for Vauxhall Pleasure Gardens, London, by the owner, Jonathan Tyers, as appropriate to a place where Handel's music 'has so often charm'd even the greatest Crouds into the profoundest Calme and most decent Behaviour'. It made the reputation of Roubiliac, who emigrated from France *c*1732 and became 18th-century England's most successful sculptor. The statue has an informality then unknown in portraits of eminent men; though Handel is shown, conventionally, playing a lyre while a cherub takes down his music, Roubiliac represents him in the nightcap and loose gown in which he composed. One of his slippers has fallen off. Oblivious to everything but music, he leans on copies of his works. The model appears especially at home in the Fitzwilliam, which owns a large collection of the composer's autograph manuscripts and his bookcase.

◄**83** Thomas Tompion (1639–
1713) and Edward Banger (*c*1668–
1720): *'Grande Sonnerie' 3-Train
Repeating Bracket Clock*,
tortoiseshell case and gilt mounts,
H 794mm. Tompion, perhaps the
greatest clockmaker of all time,
was born in Northill,
Bedfordshire, the son of the local
blacksmith. He began work in
London, probably in 1664, and
soon had a famous workshop. He
made the 'equation' clock for the
Pump Room at Bath and the two
main clocks for the Octagon Room
in the Royal Greenwich
Observatory, as well as several
clocks for the royal family. This is
an outstanding decorative
example of his work, made with his
assistant, Banger, who was his
niece's husband. The two men
parted after a quarrel in about
1708.

►**85** *Covered Tureen and Dish*,
porcelain, H 280mm, English,
Chelsea, *c*1755. It was the practice
of the Chelsea factory to auction
some of its products, and the
catalogue for the sale of 10 March
1755 describes this charming piece
as 'A most beautiful tureen in the
shape of a Hen and Chickens, big
as the life, in a curious dish
adorn'd with sunflowers'. It is one
of a number of tureens shaped like
birds, fish or animals produced by
the factory, derived in part from
examples popular at Meissen in
the 1740s. Most Chelsea examples
are *c*1753–5.

►84 William Hogarth (1697–1764): *The Bench*, oil on canvas backed on to wood, 14.8×18.2cm. This tiny painting, one of the very varied group of works by Hogarth in the Museum, is an excellent example of the artist at his most satirical. It appears to have been painted *c*1758, but a date of *c*1753 has also been proposed. Hogarth twice made an engraving after it, to which he attached a lengthy description, arguing a difference between caricature and his own method of revealing character by depicting people's appearance without (he claimed) exaggeration. It has been suggested that the picture represents actual judges of the Court of Common Pleas.

86 *Watering Can*, hybrid porcelain decorated with enamel-colours and gilt, H 250mm, L 435mm, mark: crossed batons and dots below a crown in red enamel, English, Derby, *c*1810–20. In the early 19th century Derby countered competition from other factories by producing large amounts of porcelain tableware and vases decorated with the fashionable 'Japan' patterns and other richly coloured and heavily gilt designs. Novelties were introduced, such as this full-sized watering can, now a great rarity – only one other example has so far been located (now in the Derby Museum). Miniature versions of it were still being made at Royal Crown Derby in the 1930s. The weight of the can and the holes in its lid suggest that it may have been intended as an ornamental container for pot-pourri rather than for watering flowers.

87 Pierre-Joseph Redouté (1759–1840): *Paeonia suffruticosa (Japanese Tree Peony)*, pencil and watercolour with gum arabic on prepared vellum, 466×336mm. Redouté was drawing master to Marie Antoinette, the Empress Josephine and the daughters of the Duc d'Orléans. He is famous for his beautiful drawings of flowers, made mostly as illustrations for botanical books, both other authors' and his own. This spectacular example of his art, painted in 1812 for Josephine as part of a record he compiled of the rare plants that she grew, is one of the hundreds of flower drawings, of all schools but chiefly English, French and Dutch, which Henry Broughton, 2nd Lord Fairhaven, left to the Fitzwilliam.

Pæonia Moutan. Var. B.

John Keats (1795–1821): *First Draft of 'Ode to a Nightingale'*, two sheets (only one side of the first is shown here), 205×120mm. Keats' most famous poem was written in the garden of his friend Charles Brown's house in Hampstead in May 1819. Robert Gittings, Keats' biographer, has conjectured on the evidence of this manuscript that Keats took only two sheets into the garden, where he had been regularly listening to the nightingale, because he intended to write only a short piece, but as the poem grew he was forced to cram it all on to the sheets, perhaps fearing to interrupt the process of creation by returning to the house for more paper. Keats wrote with great fluency and there are remarkably few corrections or second thoughts. In this draft the poem is entitled 'Ode to *the* Nightingale': the change to the familiar title 'Ode to *a* Nightingale' seems to have been made by Keats' publishers. The manuscript is displayed in the Museum beside a posthumous portrait of the poet by Joseph Severn and a lock of his hair cut on his deathbed in Rome by Severn. The Fitzwilliam's collection of literary manuscripts extends from the 16th century to the 20th and includes works by Blake (*An Island in the Moon*), Tennyson ('A Voice Spake out of the Skies'), Hardy (*Jude the Obscure*) and Rupert Brooke ('Grantchester').

►89 Sir Henry Raeburn (1756–1823): *William Glendonwyn*, oil on canvas, 124.8×101.6cm. Raeburn, one of the leading Scottish painters of the 18th century, recorded the personalities of Edinburgh in its 'golden age' of intellectual activity. William Glendonwyn of Glendonwyn and Sarton was married in 1781; Raeburn also painted a companion portrait of his wife and his eldest daughter, Mary. The extraordinarily beautiful golden light in which the landscape is bathed complements Raeburn's sensitive characterisation of this unassuming gentleman. The portrait dates from c1795, when Raeburn's virtuoso technique was at its height. He drew most of his portraits straight on to the canvas with a brush – he had no patience with elaborate preliminary studies or even drawings.

▲ **90** J.M.W.Turner (1775–1851): *Hospenthal, Fall of St Gothard, Sunset*, pencil, watercolour, pen and grey and purple ink, 227×286mm. This is one of a series of views near Lake Lucerne, Switzerland, that Turner painted in the early 1840s. It shows Hospenthal, near Andermatt in the pass of St Gothard; the towers of the church, dramatically enlarged, gleam in the setting sun as the shadows darken in the valley. With its sure, free style characteristic of his later years, this watercolour demonstrates Turner's genius for capturing effects of light in visions of airy intensity ('he seems to paint with tinted steam', wrote Constable). The Museum's collection of Turner watercolours spans the artist's entire career. Its nucleus is a series of 25 (of which this is one) given in 1861 by Turner's most fervent advocate, John Ruskin.

▼ **91** John Sell Cotman (1782–1842): *Dolgelly*, pencil and watercolour, 285×450mm. Cotman was born in Norwich and became the leading member of the Norwich School of landscape painters and, in his early years, a watercolourist of austere restraint. In 1802 he spent four days, from 19 to 23 July, with his sketching companion Paul Sandby Munn in Dolgelly, N Wales. This watercolour, based on a sketch made during that visit, appears to have been worked in the winter of 1804/5.

◄ **92** Samuel Palmer (1805–51): *The Magic Apple Tree*, pen, indian ink, watercolour and gum arabic, 349×273mm. In 1826 Palmer moved to the Kent village of Shoreham for the sake of his health. During the next ten years he produced his most extraordinary work there, inspired by what he called his 'valley of vision'. His depiction of the peaceful fruitfulness of the countryside is charged with a religious intensity. In this famous gouache of *c*1830 a church spire nestles in a hollow amongst fields of ripened corn, behind an apple tree laden with more fruit than nature could provide. *The Magic Apple Tree* was so called by Palmer's son, who owned it until 1928.

▲ **93** William Blake (1757–1827): *Count Ugolino and His Sons in Prison*, pen, tempera and gold on panel, 32.7×43.0cm. The Museum's large and important collection of works by Blake displays the full range of his visionary genius. This panel, one of a group of three painted in the year of his death, is a scene from Dante's *Inferno* (XXXIII, 43–75). Ugolino, with his two sons and two grandsons, was imprisoned and starved to death by his political rival in Pisa, Archbishop Ruggieri. Blake wrote to his friend Linnell in 1827 about this painting and its fellows: 'As to Ugolino, &c, I never supposed to sell them; my wife alone is answerable for their having existed in any finish'd state. I am too much attach'd to Dante to think much of anything else' – referring to his last major undertaking, an unfinished series of 102 illustrations to *The Divine Comedy*. This panel, given to the Museum by the great Blake scholar Sir Geoffrey Keynes, is based on a drawing for the series in the British Museum.

▲ **94** Jean Baptiste Camille Corot (1796–1875):
Italian Landscape, 1828, oil on paper, laid down on
canvas, 26×46cm. During the years 1825–8 Corot
was in Italy, where he spent much time painting
directly from nature. He developed an innovatory
approach to landscape which suggests form by tonal
values rather than by colour or drawing and enabled
him to capture the most subtle effects of light. This
particularly fine example of his spontaneous
approach and freedom of handling is inscribed on the
lower right 'fevrier 1828'. It is probably a view of the
coast near Naples.

▼ **95** Henri Fantin-Latour (1836–1904): *White Cup and Saucer*, oil on canvas, 19.4×28.9cm. Unlike Fantin's more usual flower pieces, portrait and figure groups or Wagnerian romances, this and a companion painting in the Fitzwilliam depicting a white candlestick are quiet and modest, and their straightforwardness and apparent simplicity recall the greatest of Dutch still-lifes of the 17th century. Fantin has been described as a 'master of white'; *White Cup and Saucer* demonstrates this to perfection.

▼ 96 George Bullock (*d*1818): *Dwarf Cabinet*, larchwood, ebony, brass mounts and boulle work, the top of Glen Tilt marble, 872× 1204×460mm, English, *c*1817. Bullock was one of the most influential furniture designers of the Regency period. His use of rich ornament gives his pieces a massive look, prefiguring Victorian taste, even when, as here, they are on a small scale.

This cabinet may have been made for the 4th Duke of Atholl at Blair Castle, Perthshire, where Bullock's firm worked 1814–19 and where two similar cabinets remain. The Duke of Atholl, called 'The Planting Duke', was well known for his interest in forestry, especially the cultivation of larch trees, and Bullock made use of wood from the Duke's plantations. His readiness to employ native materials for fashionable furniture and native plant and flower forms for decoration in place of conventional classical patterns earned him the admiration of his contemporaries, the Napoleonic wars having created a patriotic aversion to French models in art and design – which was one reason why Bullock called the very French technique of boulle work (inlay in brass) 'English buhl'.

97 John Constable (1776–1837): *Hove Beach*, oil on canvas, 33.0×50.8cm. The Fitzwilliam has a fine collection of Constable's work, in oil (both portraits and landscapes), watercolour and pencil. Constable is known to have visited Brighton several times between 1824 and 1828 for the sake of his wife's health, and this scene was painted during one of those trips. As its fresh immediacy shows, it is a study directly from nature.

98 Benedetto Pistrucci (1784–1855): *Portrait of George IV as Prince Regent*, onyx cameo, 55×39mm. Pistrucci, an Italian gem engraver and designer of medals and coins, came to London in 1815 and began a long association with the Royal Mint, becoming its Chief Medallist in 1828. He designed coins for George III and George IV and many medals, notably the one for Queen Victoria's coronation. His St George and the dragon design is familiar from its long use on English coinage. Usually his designs were carried out as wax models, while the portraits to be included were executed as cameos. This superb example was produced *c*1816 for a proposed medal to mark the British Museum's acquisition of the Elgin Marbles. The medal was never issued, but the wax models for it, and this cameo, have survived.

▲ 99 William Wyon (1795–1851): *Pattern Five Pound Piece*, Victoria (1837–1901), gold, English, London, 1839: head of Victoria/Una and the lion. William Wyon was the most distinguished artist from a family which dominated English coin and medal engraving during the 19th century. Appointed Chief Engraver at the Royal Mint in 1828, he became the first medallist to be elected to the Royal Academy (1838), a distinction here recorded in his signature on the line of the neck truncation and on the reverse. The queen's portrait is a version of the head modelled for the regular coinage and much admired by contemporaries. The reverse type, for which the Museum possesses the artist's original wax model, is a reference to Victoria's accession, two years previously, to the British throne. Wyon represents the young queen as Una, the fair princess and personification of Truth in Book I of Edmund Spenser's allegorical epic *The*

Faerie Queene (1596). During an enforced separation from her champion, the Red Crosse Knight (St George), Una is befriended and protected by a noble lion, whose fierceness turns to devotion at the sight of her beauty and purity. The climax of the Book is Una's marriage to Red Crosse, which symbolises the establishment of the Protestant Church in England. Una also represents Elizabeth I, while the lion is a familiar symbol of the British monarchy. Wyon here extends Spenser's allegory by transferring all this symbolism to his own time, identifying Una with the young Queen Victoria and the lion with her newly acquired kingdom. She guides him with her pointing sceptre, but divine direction overall is indicated by the legend DIRIGE DEUS GRESSUS MEOS, 'Guide thou, O Lord, my steps', a phrase adapted from the Old Testament, e.g. Psalm CXIX.133.

►100 Alfred Elmore (1815–51): *On the Brink*, oil on canvas, 114.3 × 83.2cm. Elmore, born in Ireland, made his reputation as a history painter. Late in his career he turned to scenes of contemporary life, often with a narrative and moral content. *On the Brink*, his first picture with a modern subject, was exhibited at the Royal Academy in 1865 and was a great popular success. It depicts the gaming tables in a fashionable German resort, probably Homburg. The title was intentionally vague. Contemporary critics assumed that the woman outside the window had lost at the tables and was being offered 'a fearful price to place her with a new chance of fortune at the table'. The hellish red glare inside contrasts with the white moonlight on her face. The passion flower, signifying susceptibility, and the lilies, signifying purity, afford a clue to the nature of the moral crisis that is taking place.

CYRIL·B·HOLMAN·HUNT   W·HOLMAN·HUNT.

◄**101** William Holman Hunt (1827–1910): *Cyril Benoni Holman Hunt*, oil on canvas, picture 60.9× 50.8cm. Holman Hunt, with Rossetti and Millais, was a founder (1848) of the Pre-Raphaelite Brotherhood and like them took as models the Italian painters before Raphael. The technique they evolved from their study of the Italian 'Primitives', employing bright colours on a wet white ground and paying meticulous attention to detail, was very influential – as was their high-minded interest in symbol and subject-matter. Of the three original founders only Hunt maintained their ideas and ideals throughout his working life. This superb example of Pre-Raphaelite portraiture shows the artist's eldest son, Cyril (1866–1934), aged 13, with his fishing rod, line and float. Cyril Benoni (his second name is Hebrew for 'child of sorrow', referring to the death of his mother, Fanny, Hunt's first wife, after his difficult birth) spent his life in the colonial service in Burma and Malaya and bequeathed this portrait to the Museum.

►**102** William de Morgan (1839–1917): *Tile Picture*, earthenware, with polychrome decoration under glaze, 873×510mm. William de Morgan was the leading English pottery designer associated with the arts-and-crafts movement: he became friendly with Burne-Jones and William Morris in the early 1860s. This tile picture was produced in the early years of the factory he founded at Fulham, London, in 1888 – a time of intense activity when he fully developed the variety of his designs and techniques. The factory made a speciality of tiles, painted either in lustre or (as here) in 'Persian colours' – the predominance of blue and turquoise is derived from de Morgan's admiration of Isnik pottery (for an example of Isnik ware in the Museum see **52**). It demonstrates his genius for creating elaborate flat patterns, in which he brought to pottery William Morris' approach to wallpaper and textile design.

▲ 103 Claude Monet (1840–1926): *Le Printemps*, oil on canvas, 64.8×80.6cm. This beautiful and characteristic work, in immaculate condition, is dated 1886. It belonged to the composer Gabriel Fauré, and it is easy to see how a painting so ravishingly pretty and so simple in its elements would have appealed to him: two girls sit in an orchard, bathed in the light that pours through the new leaves – the quintessence of spring.

▼ **104** Philip Wilson Steer (1860–1942): *Walberswick, Children Paddling*, oil on canvas, 64.2×92.4cm. Steer studied in Paris from 1882 to 1884 and, as this painting makes clear, he was much influenced by the French Impressionists. Begun *c*1890 and worked on for four years, it is one of a series of nostalgic sun-drenched beach scenes painted at Boulogne and Walberswick in the early 1890s. Such pictures have led to Steer's being dubbed an 'English Impressionist', but, as the examples of his work in the Fitzwilliam show, he was an artist of much wider range than such a label implies.

◄ **105** Edgar Degas (1834–1917): *Au Café*, détrempe on canvas, 65.7×54.6cm. This freely painted study probably dates from 1876–7. It is similar in mood and theme to three other café scenes, of which the most noted is *L'Absinthe* in the Louvre. It perfectly exhibits Degas' ability to capture fleeting subtleties of expression and gesture in rapid brushstrokes within a composition as telling and informal as a snapshot. The cutting of the right-hand figure gives a sense of great immediacy and almost uncomfortable intimacy – as if Degas were spying on the scene. It has been suggested that the subject is in fact women sewing artificial flowers on to clothes, and is to be related to Degas' series of paintings of milliners.

▲ **106** Edgar Degas (1834–1917): *Danseuse rajustant son maillot*, charcoal, 242×313mm. Degas made several similar studies of ballet dancers in this pose. The drawing formerly belonged to the Cambridge classicist A.S.F.Gow, whose purchasing of works of art was directed both by his preference for French works of the 19th century and by his wish to display what he acquired on the walls of his rooms in Trinity College for his own and others' enjoyment. Large canvases were precluded. His bequest of his collection to the Fitzwilliam is a splendid example of the Museum's enrichment by local benefactors. This sheet, squared for transfer, is one of 15 by Degas forming the nucleus of the Gow Collection.

▲ **107** Pierre-Auguste Renoir (1841–1919): *Le Coup de vent*, oil on canvas, 52.0×82.5cm. This work of *c*1873 is probably the painting that was exhibited in the first Impressionist exhibition (1874) as *Le Grand Vent*. It captures, with an effect not unlike that of a blurred photograph, the passage of a gust of wind across a landscape (probably at St Cloud). The group of paintings by Renoir in the Fitzwilliam covers all aspects of his output except portraits and nudes; *Le Coup de vent* shows what a supreme Impressionist he was.

►**108** Paul Cézanne (1839–1906): *Les Bois, Aix-en-Provence*, watercolour over black chalk, 466×300mm. One of Cézanne's later watercolours, probably of *c*1890 and painted near his birthplace, to which he had retired in 1886. It shows his deep interest in the relation between colour and light; in its analytical orderliness – so unlike Impressionism – it reveals that intense study of structure in nature which, in the hands of Picasso and Braque, led to Cubism (see **109**).

▶**110** Egon Schiele (1890–1918): *Die Freunde: Poster for the 49th Exhibition of the Vienna Secession, 1918*, colour lithograph, 635× 480mm. The Vienna Secession was an organisation formed in 1897 by a group of artists dissatisfied with the traditional teaching and appreciation of the arts in the Vienna academies. Its first president, the painter Gustav Klimt, said that its aim was to put exhibitions 'on a purely artistic footing, free from any commercial considerations . . . thereby awakening in wider circles a purified, modern view of art'. The 49th exhibition of the group was devoted to the work of Schiele and his friends. Schiele is best known for his neurotically intense portraits; this exhibition was his first major public success. He died later in the year during the great post-war influenza epidemic. The poster is derived from an unfinished painting of 1918, *Die Freunde*, and shows Schiele at the head of a table surrounded by his painter friends. The seat opposite him is occupied in the painting but empty in the poster, suggesting that the figure was Gustav Klimt, who died shortly before the exhibition opened.

▲**109** Pablo Picasso (1881–1973): *Head of a Woman*, oil on canvas, 66×53cm. Picasso painted this in Paris during the winter of 1909/10, the climax of early cubism, when for the first time he realised his aim in experimenting with a technique derived from Cézanne: to define volume without destroying the integrity of the two-dimensional picture surface and without merely imitating superficial appearances. He developed this style, known as 'analytical cubism', in close conjunction with Braque, whom he had earlier discovered struggling independently to solve the same problems. Picasso returned to the subject of a woman's head and shoulders again and again at this time, and the successful achievement of the Fitzwilliam painting, probably a portrait of his mistress Fernande Olivier, helped him to progress to the masterpieces of this period, the portraits of his friends Ambroise Vollard and Wilhelm Uhde.

SECESSION
19. AUSSTELLUNG
2-6
1K-

►**113** Walter Richard Sickert (1860–1942): *The Garden of Love*, oil on canvas, 81.9×61.6cm. A clue to this painting's subject is a drawing, also in the Fitzwilliam, of virtually the same scene, inscribed by Sickert 'Lainey's garden'. Lainey, the painter Thérèse Lessore, became Sickert's third wife in 1926. The garden can be identified as that of their house in N London. The figure is probably Mrs Sickert; the sculpture beside her is a cast of Michelangelo's Bruges *Madonna and Child*. The drawing is not squared for transfer to canvas and may be a study for a print, not the painting, though derived from the same source – probably a photograph, for by the mid 1920s Sickert had abandoned the use of preparatory drawings in favour of photographs.

▲ **111** Augustus John (1878–1961): *David and Dorelia in Normandy*, oil on canvas on millboard, 37.2×45.4cm. The figures are John's second wife, Dorelia, and his son by his first marriage, Nettleship John, always known as David. The scene is Dielette, near Cherbourg, where John and his family spent most of the summer of 1908. At this time John was experimenting with a reduced palette and simplified forms, and the luminously colourful small oil studies he painted in Normandy and Provence 1908–14 are today perhaps the most admired part of his work; the Fitzwilliam has a good collection of these as well as many examples of other aspects of his career – portraits, drawings and prints.

►**112** Charles Ricketts (1866–1931): *Pendant – 'Psyche Descending into Hell'*, enamelled gold and gemstones, H 128mm. Ricketts was a notable English *fin de siècle* painter and stage and book designer. The distinguished art collection he formed with his friend Charles Shannon was bequeathed to the Museum (see **2**). All his jewels, which were influenced by renaissance and baroque gems, were intended as gifts; this pendant was made in 1903 for the bride of his disciple and close friend, Thomas Sturge Moore.

◄**114** Paul Nash (1889–1946): *November Moon*, oil on canvas, 76.2×50.8cm. Nash was an official war artist in both world wars. A member of the Friday Club, the London Group and the New English Art Club, he exhibited at the International Surrealist Exhibitions in London in 1936 and in Paris in 1938. *November Moon*, dated 1942, is one of a group of pictures that Nash painted in the garden of his friend Hilda Harrisson's home, Sandlands, on Boar's Hill, near Oxford, between 1942 and 1944. He described them as 'transcendental'; the fungi symbolise death, the sun life and the moon fertility. The symbolism was inspired in part by Nash's reading of J.G.Frazer's *The Golden Bough*. This is the only painting of the series in which he brought together fungi and the moon.

▲ **115** Sir Stanley Spencer (1891–1959): *Self-Portrait*, oil on canvas, 32.6×55.2cm. One of a number of self-portraits painted by Spencer at intervals throughout his life. The pose clearly is derived from old-master prototypes, but this hint of traditional formality is counterbalanced by the figure of the artist jutting into the picture plane and the use of a casually rumpled bed as background. As Spencer shows himself painting with his left hand but was not left-handed, the portrait must be a single-mirror image. The Fitzwilliam owns several paintings (including another self-portrait) by this most eccentric and visionary of 20th-century British artists.

Index

(Numbers refer to illustrations)

Adoration of the Magi, alabster 43

Armour: *Helmet* 35

Bellotto, Bernardo, *Entrance to the Grand Canal* 77

Blake, William, *Ugolino and His Sons in Prison* 93

Bourdon, Sebastien, *Classical Landscape* 70

Bullock, George, *Cabinet* 96

Bushnell, John (?), *Charles II* 71

Cameo: Pistrucci, *George IV* 98

Ceramics: *earthenware*, *Nobody* 67, de Morgan, *Tile Picture* 102; *frit*, Islamic 53; *maiolica*, Dish 38; *porcelain*, Chelsea 85, Chinese 74, Derby 86, Meissen 78, Vincennes 76; *pottery*, Attic neck-amphora 12, Boeotian bell-krater 11, Cycladic vase 9; *stoneware*, Chinese box 25; *terracotta*, Attic 10, English 71, 82, Roman 20

Cézanne, Paul, *Les Bois, Aix-en-Provence* 108

Chinese: Bronze *Kuang* 26, Jade buffalo 24, Porcelain vase 74, Stoneware box 25

Classical antiquities: Bell-krater 11, Coins 15, Couch 18, Cycladic vase 9, Fountain niche 17, Gem 13, Glass 19, Marble relief 14, Neck-amphora 12, Sarcophagus 16, Terracotta 10, 20

van Cleve, Joos, *Virgin and Child* 41

Clocks and watches: Tompion and Banger, *Bracket clock* 83; Webster and Moser, *Watch and chatelaine* 81

Coins: Ancient 15, Medieval and Renaissance 37, Mogul 22, Victorian 99

Cooper, Samuel, *Lady Margaret Leigh* 51

Constable, John, *Hove Beach* 97

Corot, Jean Baptiste Camille, *Italian Landscape* 94

da Correggio, Antonio Allegri, *The Nativity* 33

Cotman, John Sell, *Dolgelly* 91

Cuyp, Aelbert, *Sunset after Rain* 64

Degas, Edward, *Au Café* 105, *Danseuse rajustant son maillot* 106

Domenico Veneziano, *The Annunciation* 32

van Dyck, Anthony, *Lucas Vorsterman* 59, *Virgin and Child* 58

Egyptian antiquities: Coffin painting 5, Mummy cartonnage 3, Portrait sculpture 4, Sketches 6, Tomb figure 2

Elmore, Alfred, *On the Brink* 100

Eworth, Hans, *Unknown Lady* 48

Fantin-Latour, Henri, *White Cup and Saucer* 95

Fitzwilliam Virginal Book 50

Fouquier, Jacques, *Winter Scene* 63

Furniture: Bullock, *Cabinet* 96

Gainsborough, Thomas, *'Heneage Lloyd and His Sister'* 80

Glass: Greenwood, *Goblet* 68, Mosque lamp 54, Syrian flask 19, Venetian tazza 39

Greenwood, Frans, *Goblet* 68

Guardi, Francesco, *Forte S. Andrea del Lido* 79

Hals, Frans, *Portrait of a Man* 62

Hilliard, Nicholas, *Earl of Southampton* 51; *Queen Elizabeth* 51

van den Hoecke, Gaspar, *Flowers* 72

Hogarth, William, *The Bench* 84

Horenbout, Lucas, *Henry VIII* 51

Hoskins, John, *Algernon Sidney (?)* 51

Hunt, William Holman, *Cyril Benoni Holman Hunt* 101

Indian: Bronze 23

Islamic: Ceramic hawk 53, Coin 22, Isnik jug 52, Mosque lamp 54, Painting of turkey 21

Jewellery: Greek gem 13, Ricketts, *Pendant*, 112

John, Augustus, *David and Dorelia in Normandy*, 111

Keats, John, *Ode to a Nightingale* 88

Liss, Johann, *A Bacchanalian Feast* 61

Lorrain, Claude, *Pastoral Landscape* 69

Manuscripts: *Fitzwilliam Virginal Book* 50, Gospel book 27, *Grey-FitzPayn Book of Hours* 30, Keats, *Ode to a Nightingale* 88

Martini, Simone, *St Geminianus* 31

Medal: Metsys, *Erasmus* 40

Medieval: Coins 37, Gold and enamel sculpture 29, Gospel book 27, *Grey-FitzPayn Book of Hours* 30, Ivory missal cover 28

Metsys, Quentin, *Erasmus* 40

Miniature paintings, Tudor and Stuart 51

Monet, Claude, *Le Printemps* 103

de Morgan, William, *Tile Picture* 102

Moser, George Michael, *Chatelaine* 81

Nash, Paul, *November Moon* 114

Nautilus cup 49

Near Eastern antiquities: Arabian lion 8, Phoenician bull 7

Needlework: English stumpwork 66

Negroli brothers (?), *Helmet* 35

Oliver, Isaac, *Henry Prince of Wales* 51

Paleolithic: Burin 1, Sketch of reindeer 1

Palma Vecchio, *Venus and Cupid* 45

Palmer, Samuel, *The Magic Apple Tree* 92

Picasso, Pablo, *Head of a Woman* 109

Pintoricchio, Bernardino, *Virgin and Child* 34

Pistrucci, Benedetto, *George IV as Prince Regent* 98

Raeburn, Henry, *William Glendonwyn* 89

Redouté, Pierre-Joseph, *Paeonia suffruticosa* 87

Rembrandt van Rijn, *Jacob Shown the Coat of Joseph* 60

Renoir, Pierre-Auguste, *Le Coup de vent* 107

Riccio (Andrea Briosco), *Head of a Ram* 36

Ricketts, Charles, *Pendant – 'Psyche'* 112

Riza-i'Abbasi, *Bagpipe Player* 55

Roubiliac, Louis François, *G.F.Handel* 82

Rubens, Peter Paul, *The Death of Hippolytus* 57, *Head of a Bearded Man* 56

van Ruysdael, Salomon, *Farm Buildings* 65

Schiele, Egon, *Die Freunde* 110

Sickert, Walter Richard, *The Garden of Love* 113

Silver: French basin 42, Isnik jug mounts 52, Nautilus cup mounts 49

Spencer, Stanley, *Self-Portrait* 115

Steer, Philip Wilson, *Walberswick* 104

Titian, *Tarquin and Lucretia* 47, *Venus and Cupid with a Luteplayer* 46

Tompion, Thomas, and Edward Banger, *Bracket clock* 83

Turner, J.M.W., *Hospenthal, Fall of St Gothard* 90

Utamaro, *Parody of Chūshingura* 73

Veronese, Paolo, *Hermes, Herse and Aglauros* 44

Watteau, Antoine, *Man Playing the Flute* 75

Wright of Derby, Joseph, *The Hon. Richard Fitzwilliam* frontispiece

Wyon, William, *Pattern five pound piece* 99